What Brothers Think,
What Sistahs Know

Also by Denene Millner

The Sistahs' Rules

What Brothers Think, What Sistahs Know

The Real Deal on Love and Relationships

Denene Millner
and her husband, **Nick Chiles**

William Morrow and Company, Inc.
New York

The poem on page 40 is from *Black Feeling, Black Talk, Black Judgement* by Nikki Giovanni © 1968 by Nikki Giovanni. Reprinted by permission of Willam Morrow and Company, Inc.

It is the policy of William Morrow and Company, Inc., and its imprints and affiliates, recognizing the importance of preserving what has been written, to print the books we publish on acid-free paper, and we exert our best efforts to that end.

Library of Congress Cataloging-in-Publication Data
Millner, Denene.
    What brothers think, what sistahs know : the real deal on love and relationships / Denene Millner and Nick Chiles.
        p.   cm.
    ISBN 0-688-16498-6
    1. Man-woman relationships.   2. Afro-American women.   3. Afro-American men.   4. Love.   5. Intimacy (Psychology)   I. Chiles, Nick.   II. Title.
    HQ801.M5753   1999
    306.7'089'96073—dc21   98-30617
                                                                                    CIP

Printed in the United States of America

First Edition

1 2 3 4 5 6 7 8 9 10

BOOK DESIGN BY RENATO STANISIC

www.williammorrow.com

For the couples who have shown us through word and deed what it means to live and love in another's space—and how wonderful it is to get along in it.

Migozo and Chikuyu Chiles
Bettye and Jimmy Millner
Angelou and James Ezeilo
Desere and Shawn Dove
Bethsheba Cooper and James O'Neal

and us

Contents

♥

Introduction

We'd first like to say what we are *not*. We are *not* psychiatrists or psychologists or social workers or anybody else who gets paid by the hour (or partial hour) to step into the mind with a Dustbuster and clear away the accumulated junk. We are *not* spokespersons for the race, angling for a slot on *Nightline* to tell Ted what the other forty million black people had for breakfast. We are *not* offering the definitive word on black love that will shut down any further conversation on the subject. We are *not* by a long shot presuming to speak for every black man and every black woman.

What we are doing in these pages is talking. We think that's one of the most important things we can do as two black people in love: Talk. Talk about the soothing, sexy stuff that brothers and sistahs whisper to each other when the lights are turned off and the juices start flowing; talk about the hard, divisive stuff that enrages us—white girls, sistahs' unappealing attitudes, brothers' obsessive focus on appearance.

At a memorable forum in Philadelphia last year at the Black Writers Workshop, when brothers and sistahs came together to talk and complain about each other, we witnessed the depth of feeling in our community on this topic. Both sides desperately wanted to be heard, and we quickly realized how seldom brothers and sistahs come together to air their grievances and learn from each other. When we began to talk, we noticed something happening: we recognized that we had never heard these questions answered truthfully by the opposite sex; we started learning things about each other. Similar scenes were repeated all over the country during the book tour for *The Sistahs' Rules.*

We decided this book was a way to keep the discussion going.

Every relationship is neverending exploration, but many of us never get around to asking those tough questions whose answers inform everything that will follow and sometimes even make us change our behavior. Men and women rarely get a chance to look at the world through each others' eyes, to introduce empathy and understanding into our interactions. Instead we tend to yell and talk at each other without listening. As a consequence, many of us suffer through one painful relationship after another, never understanding why the men never won't the ring on that left hand or the women keep running away.

How much better off we would all be if, when we turned thirteen, our parents could stroll over to the bookshelf and hand us a Survival Guide to Understanding the Other. Throughout our teen years, every date would be a road test for our Survival Guide, and we'd begin decoding the inscrutable ways of the opposite sex.

By the time we reached twenty-one, our skills would be incisor-sharp. We'd be able to tell exactly when a woman is flirting or when her smile is actually a grimace of pain, if a man really does want to listen to our problems with our boss, why so many men could run down Michael Johnson in an effort to escape commitment, how come a woman starts to practice writing the man's last name and a hyphen after one date.

But, alas, there is no such Survival Guide. Nothing even close to it. We're lucky if our parents warn us about the approach of armpit hair.

With no such guide, no primer, we all stumble into adulthood with no clue and no idea where to find one. But, as unequipped and blind as we are, we still rush out there groping around for a partner. Sometimes we get lucky and bump into someone with whom we can actually vibe, a real soulmate. Sometimes we aren't as lucky and our groping hands happen upon the waiting mouth of a pit bull—we can only hope we still have a few digits left when the relationship is over. Dating is like playing a game without a rule book. Is there any wonder, in the midst of such raging ignorance and unpreparedness, that black men and women have problems communicating with each other?

Imagine if foreign sociologists landed on the shores of the United States and wanted a quick peek into the state of black love. All they'd need to do is find any sistah possessing a full complement of limbs and most of her teeth and follow her down the street. In a matter of moments, maybe seconds, the researchers would start collecting hard evidence that there's a problem—loud, noisy kisses would be lobbed at the woman by strange men; boisterous shouts from stairwells and street corners would, in quick succession, compliment the woman on the roundness of her ass, ask her out on a date, then assault her with angry curses when she didn't respond. The researchers might rush up to the men and ask, "Is this odd form of courtship ever successful?" The men would have to say, "No." They'd ask: "Do the women appear to be pleased?" The men would have to say, "No." They'd ask: "Would you approve of this being done to the women with whom you share a familial bloodline?" The men would say, "No." The researchers would have no choice but to ask: "Then why the hell did you do that?" They'd probably get a whole lot of silence in response. But if those men had been handed a guide at thirteen, it would have told them, in no uncertain terms: "Leering and shouting at a woman on the street does NOT turn her on."

Follow these same researchers into a nightclub frequented by black men and women. On the surface, things are promising—the dance floor is packed with sexy bodies undulating to the slammin' beat. But then the researchers would be well advised to select a decent-enough-looking fellow and trail him around the club. Watch him pick out an attractive woman sitting by herself in the corner, dancing in her chair. He walks up and immediately her face goes into scowl mode. He doesn't even have the whole question out of his mouth—"Excuse me, would you like to . . ."—before she spits an unpleasant "No" back at him. He approaches another, then another, and always gets the same answer: "No." Head hanging, he goes back to his wall and for the rest of the night curses every woman in the club under his breath. The curious researchers might want to ask a few of these women, "Why wouldn't you dance with that fellow?" They might respond, "Shee-it. I don't know him." The follow-up question would likely be: "Then why the hell are you here?" How might these women have been helped by a Survival Guide? Simple. At the age of thirteen, they would have been told: "Don't go to a nightclub without a man if you are repulsed by strange men."

We want this book to be a Survival Guide of sorts—a document that sheds some light on what the other half is thinking. If you read this book, you won't lose sleep anymore trying to get into each other's head. We're gonna do it for you. You will better understand the other and make more informed choices. And you will talk to each other.

What Brothers Think,
What Sistahs Know

♥

Prologue

If you really, really want to get to know your partner, try writing a book together.

Over the course of three months, we had to hash out our feelings on some pretty dicey topics before we began to put fingers to the keyboard. (Ask your partner how he or she would react if you got fat and see what happens.) It wasn't always pleasant, it wasn't always easy, but it certainly was informative. We learned things about ex-boyfriends and ex-girlfriends that we probably didn't need to know; we heard some closely held views that we weren't pleased to hear. But in the end, even though we didn't always agree, the process of talking and writing drew us even closer together.

Denene usually composed on the laptop, on which she pounded away as she sat in front of the television. (Hey, whatever works.) Nick wrote on the desktop, hunched over the keyboard in the tiny office/computer room. Our meeting point was often the kitchen, where we'd munch on snacks—Cheezits, Häagen-Dazs, cold leftover chicken wings—we shouldn't be eating and argue or clarify one point after another. When the exchanges between us on paper and face-to-face got particularly testy on a few occasions, we'd stay in our neutral corners and hit the kitchen when the other person wasn't there.

But even if the conversation on these rare days was strained, we still had to talk to get the work done. That turned out to be a healthy experience for us, because, like many couples, we had always found it easier to inflict silence on each other when there was a chill in the air.

Of course, advising couples to "communicate" has got to be some of the oldest advice under the sun. That doesn't necessarily mean it's not sage advice—it's just not very original. But knowing that you should talk to each other and doing it are very different things, aren't they? That's where we hope this book will come in handy. Perhaps you can use the topics we selected and the questions we posed as starting points, initiating a dialogue by asking your man or woman how they would answer our questions and whether they agree or disagree with the answers we gave. Perhaps you could ask your mate whether some of the solutions we offer would work in your household. Or maybe you can just try some of our suggestions and see for yourself whether they work. (One exception: the advice about rubbing out your man's momma is a joke. If you don't recognize that, you got problems we can't help you with.)

If you do use this book in any way to initiate dialogue or just to make your partner laugh, we'd like to hear about it. Share your stories with us. Write us at

William Morrow and Company Inc.
1350 Avenue of the Americas
New York, NY 10019

The Meeting Stage

CHAPTER 1

Yoo-hoo! Over Here: How Do We Get Your Attention?

From a Sistah

Can't count how many times I've been to a party with a bunch of beautiful sistahs, dip from head to toe, smelling good, sweet as sweet potato pie and ready to tear up the rug and expecting to tuck a few cuties' numbers into their purses by the end of the night—and they end up leaving dejected, having spent a full two hours buying themselves their own drinks and dancing in a circle with their girlfriends.

The cuties are there—dressed to kill and sipping their Henny, standing up against the wall next to their boys, simultaneously doing the two-step and surveying the room. But they don't move from that spot—unless it's to get a refill on that Courvoisier. They don't dance with anyone, except the wall and the one weave-and-leather-wearing-big-booty-spiked-heel woman in the room who looks like she's a little hot in the ass. And they hardly strike up a conversation with anyone other than their boys.

And in the meantime, we sistahs are left to feel like the wicked stepsister at the ball—unattractive, out of shape, just plain unworthy.

We thought we'd done everything we were supposed to do to get a guy interested in us. We made sure we looked cute that night. Threw a casual glance over at Mr. Two-Step—might have even tossed the booty in his direction.

Alas, no play.

No forseeable action.

Forced to go home feeling woefully inadequate—like we don't have what it takes to snag a good one.

It's a harrowing experience.

Ditto for the cute brother on the subway who sees us every morning at the same exact time at the same exact place, but ignores our behinds every single solitary day—and the cute guy at the video store, grocery store, mall, hell, anywhere we go where there are fine guys to whom we might be inclined to give some play.

Now maybe it's us—and we're sure you'll correct us if we're wrong—but it doesn't seem like brothers are into that old-fashioned way of meeting a sistah—the one where he sees a woman and, like, talks to her. Offers to buy her a glass of wine. Asks her out on a date.

It's almost as if we don't exist.

What do we have to do to attract your attention and get you to approach us?

From a Brother

Hold up; wait a minute. You're kidding, right? Because that scenario you've painted doesn't exist in any world I've inhabited. Where are these pretty, put-together sistahs just waiting to give all these brothers some play? This is surely a figment of your vivid imagination, right?

Let me give you this scenario as a reality check: We're leaning against the wall in the club with our boys, checking out all the cuties gathered in tight little circles with their girlfriends. We assume these women are at a DANCE club to DANCE. I don't think that's an outrageous assumption to make. We were excited and anxious when we got there because there were so many beautiful women in the house. We survey the scene carefully, trying to pick out the right one to approach. This is a dangerous, careful science. Make a mistake and our experiment blows up in our face, right there in front of the whole club. We are looking for a sign from anything with breasts. She must be with a group of three women or less so that our embarrassment will be kept to a minimum if we get dissed. She must look warm and fairly happy about life. This means that at some point we see a smile cross her lips. She must have hit the dance floor at some point during the course of the evening. If she has thrown a glance in our direction, all the better—but this one isn't entirely necessary (maybe she just can't see us from where she's sitting). We take about two hundred deep breaths, we maybe do a quick shot of Jack to boost our confidence, then we march across that interminable stretch of dance floor separating us from her table, we present ourselves in front of her and we let the magic words slide from our lips: "Would you like to dance?"

Invariably what we get in these situations is a very quick and decisive, "No, not now." That, of course, is the same as, "Hell no, Negro, now get out my way!" Though we try not to make it appear so, we are shattered. We walk back to our spot against the wall. Our boy, if he's truly our boy, offers a few mumbled curses in our behalf thrown in her direction. Maybe we get the nerve to try this one or two more times, but after awhile, thoroughly defeated and confused, we give up. In the bathroom, we stare at ourselves in the mirror and wonder what's wrong. Does our breath stink? Is there a large booger in our nose? Is it the color of the suit? (Maybe she doesn't like purple.) The haircut?

This happens all the time. It happens so often that we really don't understand what you're talking about when you complain about men not asking you to dance. It is truly a case of the genders looking at the same issue from perspectives as far apart as Mississippi and the motherland. Recently I was at a club with my wife, my sister Angelou and a group of her female friends who all happen to be single. The single women occasionally all danced together in a circle, looking like they were enjoying themselves. But then they'd sit down and look around the club, waiting—or so I thought. Then a man approached one of the women and asked her to dance. Immediately, she said, "No." Just like that. Wouldn't you know it—the next day this woman was complaining about not meeting any men at the club. Typical.

And forget about the subway, the grocery store or the video store—no way in hell you're giving us play in these locations. Come now—how many times have you really been willing to give some stranger play on the subway? Yeah, you might give him a smile if he's exceptionally good-looking; you might even let him talk to you. But are you really going to give this stranger a phone number or the necessary information to allow him to find you once you step off the train? I think not. I think sistahs step out the door with that Hannibal Lecter mask on, and it takes rare and exceptional circumstances for the average brother to pry it off.

You wonder why the sistah with the weave, big booty and the spiked heels is getting all the dances and all the play? Well, for one, if she has a big booty and she's out there on the dance floor twirling it around for every brother to see, we're probably going to be lining up to get our chance to bask in its glorious rays. As for the weave, most brothers tend to care about or notice these hair issues much less than the sistahs do. If this sistah looks like she's having a good time and she's likely to dance with us, we're certainly going to give her a shot—particularly if the booty's talking to us. You're all going to look at her attributes and her clothes and figure we're shallow and superficial for going after her.

But what you all conveniently ignore is her attitude.

The sistah is enjoying herself; *she looks like fun.* This is what the brothers came to the club looking for: FUN. So we're going to be drawn to this sistah like flies on . . . well, you know.

Why do you all get dolled up and travel en masse with your girls to the dance club if you don't want to dance? What—or, more specifically, who—are you waiting for? Surely you know Denzel doesn't hit the clubs anymore.

From a Sistah

Ha-ha—very funny. Yes, we like to get our little grooves on as much as guys do on the dance floor—we'll whip off our heels and cut a rug into shreds if you give us a minute. And if a cheap Denzel knockoff asks us to dance, watch out! We're ready to get that soul clap going and sing right along with Frankie Beverly when he gets to that "Before I let you goooo, oooh-oh ooooh. Oh, I will never never never never never never never never let you go before I go" in "Before I Let You Go." But only if he looks like he's not going to give us any static.

That's right. Static.

Y'all sistahs know what I'm talking about. It's the static that comes when Denzel Fake-ington decides that just because we told him we would dance with him it gave him the right to feel up every moving body part on our frame that his two hands can reach.

That's right: A sistah who says "yes" to a brother and takes his hand as he leads her onto the dance floor knows that a good 80 percent of the time, she better step to the dance floor prepared to pull some boxing gloves out of her bra and take on the brute strength of Mike Tyson if all she wants to do is dance.

You brothers know who you are.

We watch you work the room, going from sistah to sistah to sistah until one poor fool gets caught moving too much on a good song and you push up in just the precise second she was *really* feeling the beat and she said, "Sure, I'll dance with you." And as soon as girlfriend gets out of the two-step, dips, turns and tosses you a little booty? Oh my God, you lose your mind, throw your hands in the air and zero in for the kill—groin to booty, gyrating and twisting and sweating and stuff all over her good suit. Had you two been naked, she'd have left the floor eight weeks pregnant.

It's embarrassing as hell—you acting like a fool, connected to her backside. She tries to push you off, but you act like that's just part of her dance routine—until another song comes on and she runs terrified from the dance floor, eyes darting around the room to see just who all saw her getting felt up like a two-dollar ho in front of the entire nightclub. And he has the nerve—no, the outright audacity—to ask her for the digits as she dashes.

And trust me, every woman in the joint's done peeped it—including the thirty other ladies who refused your hand before you got to her.

Now, do you really think I'm going out like that? *Hell no!*

We sistahs would rather dance with our girls than get caught boogeying with some guy who's going to think that our two-step is his license to rub his little thing all over us.

See, when we go to the club, we do want to dance—we do want to have a good time. But we want to be respected, too. We want the man to be a gentleman—to ask us politely if we would like to dance, to keep a respectful distance from us while we're on the dance floor and to say "thank you" after it's over—without pressuring us into standing over by the bar and telling him our life story as he "please baby, please baby, please baby, baby, pleases" his way through his request for the digits, or, worse yet, an after-the-club date.

We just want to dance—and, perhaps, assess the chemistry from a healthy distance.

If we hit it off, then cool—we'll talk to you. And it might

actually result in the exchanging of phone numbers. But if we just want an innocent dance—one with no strings (or groins) attached, respect that. Then maybe we'll be more inclined to accept that dance card.

Speaking of dance cards: What would you think if we asked you for a dance—or, better yet, out on a date—after we showed you love up in the club?

From a Brother

First, we'd fall to the floor and kiss your feet—granted they looked well-scrubbed and relatively corn-free. Then we'd stand up, give you a gracious bow in honor of your wisdom and foresight, and say, "Hell yeah, I'll go out with you!"

These are the kinds of questions that brothers don't understand. Why would we have a problem with a woman asking us out on a date, as long as we were available and interested? It relieves us of the pressure and possibility of getting dissed.

When I was in elementary school, it was common practice for girls to write those little notes to boys they liked, asking the boys to check the "yes" or "no" box to indicate whether they liked the note-writer in return. Sometimes the note even got passed to the object of the girl's affections through another intermediary, a friend of the boy. But the point was that it eventually got there, it announced the girl's intentions and feelings, and it made the boy a happy little dude for the rest of that day and probably that week. (Of course, little boys being little boys, he may not have always had the proper response. He might've decided that he didn't want to be so transparent about his answer, so he might've started a fight with her or thrown her in the mud first to camouflage his extreme pleasure.)

So, what happened to all that elementary schoolgirl aggression? What killed it over the years? Was it this notion that men liked to be the aggressors, the pursuers—a notion furthered by women such as those who wrote that book *The Rules*?

I'm here to announce that although some men may tell you they like to be the aggressors, there's likely not a man in the world who isn't thrilled by the idea of a woman making the first move. (Unless your name happens to be Michael Jordan or Wesley Snipes, both of whom probably get nauseated by all the luscious beauties throwing themselves at them. Tough life.)

We can't repeat enough that we're just as frightened by getting dissed in a club as you're all frustrated because not enough of us ask you to dance. There's a major problem here, a logjam that won't be broken unless somebody is bold enough to make the first move. I wish more men could toss their feelings and their egos to the side and approach every woman in the club for a dance. But you know how that would look. That brother would soon become a clubwide joke as the crowd witnessed the rejections start to pile up. In the absence of bigger male *cojones,* we need some help from the females. More aggression on your part would go far in breaking the logjam. Who knows—some of y'all might even find husbands.

But I ask of you, please, be realistic. If you know you're no Halle Berry, if you have more in common with bassett hound than Angela Bassett, don't march up to the best-looking brother in the club and expect him to be thrilled by your invitation. If he's a nice guy, he might agree to dance with you, but he's not going to be wild about spending the rest of the evening with you at his side, chasing away all the cuties. This is shallow and evil, you say? (See Chapter 3 on the importance of appearance.) I offer in evidence Exhibit A: The devastating ugliness that ensues when the pudgy brother with the bad teeth and nonexistent rap saunters up to Fly Girl, interrupting her love affair with her vanity mirror, and asks her to join him on the dance floor. Are onlookers more likely to say Fly Girl was shallow, or to ask themselves what in the world could Brotherman have been thinking?

The Huff and Puff Syndrome: Why Do Brothers Think All Sistahs Are Mad?

From a Sistah

Frankly, we're tired of it.

Tired of the notion that we, at the drop of a dime, will snap our fingers, roll our necks, suck our teeth and read people—particularly brothers—from head to toe for any transgression, with little regard for folks' feelings. I once interviewed NBA player Ray Allen about his starring role in Spike Lee's movie, *He Got Game,* and we got into a lively discussion on why so many black men appear to be rejecting black women. I told him that it seemed as if black men stood on line waiting for their chance to knock sistahs down and step over their prone, bleeding bodies to get to the white girl. He defended the brothers with a spirited argument about how they tire of black women who seem "quick to throw a hand in your face and walk away." Allen even went so far as to say that white women are easier to deal with than sistahs because white girls just "want to have fun" and that it's easier to deal with a white woman who "sticks by you" rather than a black woman who works hard to try to "make something of herself" and "won't take any mess."

I wasn't aware that trying to succeed in life and refusing to tolerate other people's crap were bad traits to have, but hey—who are we to judge? We're simply trying to get to the bottom of why brothers think the way they do.

We sistahs would be remiss if we tried to pretend that Ray's assessment of us didn't have some element of truth to it. Some of us are extremely motivated, and a few of us do tend to mercilessly break folks down under the misguided notion that folks need to be broke. I remember this one sistah who, at my very first book signing for *The Sistahs' Rules,* made a point of sitting right up in the front of the audience—arms folded, lips twisted all up on the side of her face, bass in her voice—so that she could lob her "your book is shallow because black men just can't hang and you don't address their insecurities and how they can't deal with a strong-minded, independent, successful black woman like me" question. Her statement was ugly and her attitude even uglier—making it more than a little bit clear why homegirl was having problems finding a man: Her problems began at home. She was angry, and it was obvious that it was going to take way more than my simple, matter-of-fact, pat answers to clear up whatever problems she was having with men.

Yes, there are plenty of other women like her—sistahs who lug their old bones in baggage that they readily foist on others, particularly brothers, to soothe whatever pain they're carrying around in their hearts.

But that's only *some* sistahs.

In the meantime, the rest of us suffer because of the mean indiscretions of a few. Some black men accuse us of being emasculating bitches, while others claim we collude with white men to take the best jobs, the best titles and the best salaries away from them. And we sistahs wonder how in the hell we got there, seeing as we know you know nobody in this whole wide world goes out of her way more to love, protect and respect black men than black women—even when our brothers have their left feet on our necks.

Still, here we sistahs stand, accused of giving brothers a disgustingly hard time. What we sistahs really want to know is why brothers always paint us with the same maddening stroke.

Where did you all get the idea that we're all mean and angry?

From a Brother

From eating, sleeping, and breathing black women from the day we were born—that's where. The thoughts you expressed in your question sounded to me like a thorough description of the angry sistahs who frighten us and make us wary of the whole lot of you.

Does the following sistah sound familiar?

On the outside, she looks perfectly normal. She might even be gorgeous. She has all the right clothes, drives a nice car, always has the hair coiffed to perfection, is steadily climbing the career ladder, maybe even skipping a few rungs on the way up. But there's a problem. She has been unlucky at love.

Actually, unlucky may not be the right word. She has been disastrous at love. Her past relationships have folded like a house of cards. She is not happy about this. And she is intent on blaming every brother she encounters. With one hostile glance, she presumes to know everything about us, down to the length of time it'll take us to cheat on her, the lack of table manners we will demonstrate at those fancy restaurants she loves, and the reaction we will have when we find out how much money she makes.

Unfortunately, this description fits far too many women in the African-American community. They walk around flashing their anger for all to see, especially the brothers. Try approaching them or even saying "Hi" and you better duck. Forget about talking to one of them on the street. In public, sistahs seem to assume that every brother on the planet is an ax murderer in disguise if we try to utter a word to them. Sure, many brothers spend much of their days tossing out some of the vilest, rudest, nastiest comments to every woman they encounter in the strange hope that she will give them some play—and then when they're ignored the brothers can turn on the sistahs like a dim-witted bully who's just been slapped. But that's certainly not an apt description for every brother, or even most brothers.

The fact that our women no longer even bother to make such distinctions is bothersome. We expect it from the police—but not our own. As you so eloquently stated above, "But that's only *some* . . . In the meantime, the rest of us suffer because of the mean indiscretions of a few." What we have here is a failure to communicate.

In talking to brothers, it is the chief complaint I hear, over and over: black women are too damn evil. That certainly doesn't apply to all black women, but the Evilenes surely are plentiful.

Apparently many of them have forgotten one of Mom's early lessons: You attract more flies with honey than vinegar.

What these women fail to understand is that we're just as human as they are. Why would we subject ourselves to their abuse if we didn't have to? If there's a sweet, warm, lovely woman sitting next to her in church or in the movie theater or the club, why would we waste our time with her when she's likely only to give us grief? We're going to move past her to the next one, the woman smiling at us and behaving as if she actually wants to spend some time with us. Just like anybody else, we like to be around nice people. People who don't insult us. People who don't make us feel bad about ourselves. People who don't try to dis us in front of our friends and family. People who don't snicker when we tell them what we do for a living. People who don't throw their accomplishments in our faces like an accusation.

Not all of us feel like Ray Allen, however. And we don't all rush out to find white girls because we've met a few nasty sistahs. In fact, the overwhelming majority of us don't do this. We know we need a partner who is going to confront with us those unpleasantries that are thrown in black people's faces in a steady drumbeat of ugliness; a partner who will retrieve our souls when they have been bruised and battered and who will give us enough strength and love to pick ourselves up and dust ourselves off to face all those Mondays. Yes, we go out there and brace ourselves for perhaps a few more unpleasant encounters per week with the hope that one day Miss Ebony Sunshine is going to come strolling into our lives. If I had let my past experiences with angry black women sour me on all the black women I had yet to meet, I wouldn't have been in the proper mindset to appreciate the happy, cheerful beauty of my darling wife.

But we still wonder why there has to be such an undercurrent of hostility in our interactions. Will we ever find peace?

And if you're going to treat every brother you pass on the street as if he's lower than a sewer rat, have we now reached the point where black men shouldn't even bother trying to speak to black women in public?

From a Sistah

Okay, we admit it: It is extremely difficult for a lot of us women to avoid assuming the worst when we meet a black man—especially under everyday circumstances, like on the street or the train or anywhere public, for that matter.

The actions of your kind dictate that. "Yo, yo, choc'late— whassup wit' dem digits"—a phrase that all too often finds its way from the lips of strange men yelling out to us on the street, on the bus, on the subway, hell, anywhere—tends to have a profound effect on how we sistahs perceive black men—particularly when it's followed up with the "B" word if we ignore his stupid behind and, like CeCe Peniston, "keep on walkin'." Still, brothers hit us with it—while we're on our way to work, when we're with our babies or our mamas or our girlfriends. Over and over again, complete strangers who should be respecting us with a "Mornin', sistah, how you doin' today?" have, instead, treated us like we're pieces of whiting to be bargained over at the local fish store—and we've pushed past them, taken our insults with pursed lips and furrowed brows, and gone on about our business, mad as hell that yet another brother felt it necessary to embarrass the shit out of us.

News flash: Public degradation and humiliation from a complete stranger is the quickest way to send a sistah running and screaming in the opposite direction. Ditto for the guy who just walked the length of the club whispering in every ear attached to a person with boobs, his pocket bulging with little white pieces of paper full of phone numbers. Comments and actions like these make us feel cheap and disrespected—like a piece of meat, rather than a person who is worthy of the courtesy and kindness that you would show someone you were trying to get to know better.

And, unfortunately, fools like that make the rest of you suffer.

It's sort of like the perception white folks get of you guys by watching the evening news: You know, see a black guy, remember the big black dude who was paraded across the screen last night in handcuffs, clutch your pocketbook, hope someone else steps into the elevator and saves you from attack. Well, that's the way it pretty much works with us when it comes to black men. We've been dogged out, disrespected, unprotected and hung out to dry so many times that we just assume the worst is to come when the next one of your lot approaches. We don't know what to expect: Is he going to insult me? Is he going to cuss me out? Is he crazy and deranged and looking to hurt me? It's not easy to get past that, day in and day out.

Neither is it easy to get rid of the baggage we've collected from the brothers of our past. You know the deal: One brother cheats, you all cheat. Another brother takes us out for a great time, then stops returning phone calls, you all play games. Face it: You've all gathered a pretty good reputation for playing just a little too much—and we've carefully guarded our hearts with our Fort Knox.

That's not to say you're all playas; it's just to say we've grown accustomed to not trusting. You get slapped enough times, you learn to duck when you think the next smack is coming. It's human nature—sistah nature.

We sistahs also learn pretty quickly to put up our dukes when we recognize brothers are giving us some play not because they're actually interested in getting to know us as people, but because they're too busy looking at our body parts. Most sistahs will dis you in a heartbeat if you make it painfully obvious that the only reason you're talking to her is for carnal pleasures. She can spot you out like jheri curl juice on a white pillowcase.

Perhaps brothers would do well to stop being so obvious.

We don't want you to stop approaching us; we just want you all to change up your strategy. Instead of looking at her breasts and behind and legs while you're saying, "Good morning, sistah," perhaps it would go over better if you looked her in the eye with a little respect—afforded her some dignity, gave her a reason to want to speak back to you.

And if she doesn't speak to you, recognize that it's no slight to you if she doesn't respond to your respectful "Hello"—that it's not something to take personally. Perhaps she just had a bad day; maybe the boss pissed her off to the highest of pisstivity, or her sister soiled her good white skirt, or she just didn't hear you when you said, "Good morning." It doesn't always have to be so damn personal.

In the meantime, what can we sistahs do to get you brothers

to get past this notion that God put us here on this earth expressly to make brothers miserable?

From a Brother

Let's start with a little humanity. I bet a lot of sistahs would be kinder to a stray cat than they are to most black men they encounter on the street. What we're looking for is that old-style, black-on-black bond that black people used to share when they saw each other on the street. You know, the "How do you do" and "Have a nice day" comments that black people used to pass back and forth to each other, usually accompanied by a smile.

I understand that for this to happen, brothers will bear a large part of the responsibility. You don't need to tell me that you don't get a lot of "How do you do" greetings from brothers on the street. But sistahs have gotten to the point where they treat a simple "hi" like it's the same as "Hey, bitch."

To seal the deal, all we gotta do is get to that one trifling, snaggletooth, nasty-ass brother on the corner. Y'all know him. So if any readers out there happen to be acquainted with that brother, if he's your long-lost cousin Pookie or Uncle Ray-Ray, please show him this chapter. Or maybe you'll need to read it to him. And tell him he's jacking up the flow for the entire black male population.

How Much Does Appearance Really Count?

From a Sistah

Hey—you remember that commercial, the one where these two women are standing by the bar with a male friend they've decided to set up on a date with one of their girls, and the girl gets stuck somewhere and can't make it and ol' boy is like, "Oh, that's too bad—but, um, what does she look like?"

Guys hoot and holler over that one, nod their heads furiously in agreement. And we women are like, "God, could he be any more superficial?"

For us, it's personality. Is the guy sweet and kind and gentle and honest? That's what we want to know. He may not be the cutest thing on this earth, but we'll treat him like gold if he's got all that other stuff going for him. And don't let him have some money, a career and a little public spotlight. Could be so ugly you want to smack his momma, but all is forgiven and dismissed if he's got a little something in his pocket and his heart.

But dudes? Huh. No such luck. If she's not Vanessa Williams or some runway type, she can forget the initial hookup—unless, of course, it comes at the end of the night in the club, when guys are most desperate to make sure they don't go home alone that Jamie Foxx's "Wanda" from *In Living Color* could get some play. But let it be daylight. Let her be cute but not fine. Let him take a good look in her face and, just when he's convinced himself she's cute enough to talk to, let a cuter woman pass by. Watch his smoke. For guys it's like, Personality what? Sweet who? What you say about her treating me right, being talented, having money and a career, her availability? "Oh, that's nice—um, what does she look like?" he'll ask with bated breath, completely oblivious to his obviousness.

Can you spell s-h-a-l-l-o-w?

We can't knock a brother's hustle; if he's in the market for a fine young thang, then cool—we can understand that, kinda. But must *every* brother be on the hunt for Halle Berry? Must every woman have a 36–24–36 brick house body with a Lisa Nicole Carson face in order to get some play? I've listened to my brother and my male friends ogle pretty women and dis the average-looking sistahs—even heard the not-so-cute ones referred to as "booger bears" by a few of the guys. And those kinds of comments aren't just coming from the lips of handsome men; a brother could be average or, worst yet, a booger bear himself, and he'll still find it necessary to rank on a sistah's looks—as if Halle would wait, panting, for him to come knocking on her door.

What's up with that? Why do you guys harp so much on appearance?

From a Brother

Don't front, dearie; everybody harps on appearance. We're just less willing to look past it than you females are, that's all.

There's a reason that we can't take our eyes off a person whom we find extremely attractive. From birth, we're fitted with a chip that allows us to appreciate beauty in its stunning variety of forms—whether it's the majesty of a crashing waterfall, the fierce countenance of a Bengal tiger, the intimidating brilliance of a sunset, or the graceful curves of the female form. We know beauty when we see it, and we want to look at it and touch it and kiss it and be around it as much as we possibly can. We will go to far extremes to surround ourselves with beauty; it inspires us, it makes us feel better about ourselves—it may even make us feel happy.

No one frowns when a man travels halfway around the world to view the Taj Mahal or the Amazonian rain forest, but let us pick a pretty girl over a plain one for a dance or a date and we become the most heartless, boorish creatures ever to walk the earth. It's almost counterintuitive to expect a man, a dog, a donkey or any other creature to choose the uninspiring over the inspiring, the droll over the spectacular, the humdrum over the heart-stopping. We're just not built that way.

Of course, there are circumstances when our decisionmaking becomes a bit more complicated. For instance, if we think the beauty is clearly out of our league, we're going to go for the plain to avoid utter embarrassment and unpleasant scenes. We're going to seek someone closer to our own level. Unfortunately, many of us don't have an accurate reading of what our level is. Some of us have calculated our level as much too high; others have under-played their hand and placed their level way too low.

We know that women have a different set of priorities from us. We see it all over the gossip pages and the supermarket tab-loids whenever we spot a gorgeous woman with an ugly guy. We immediately know she picked him for a reason other than his looks—money, status, power. In other words, she could look past his appearance and fasten onto some other attribute.

Women often ask whether we care about a woman's "person-ality." But as you ladies all know, we've been trained to look around suspiciously when we hear the word "personality" 'cause that's the international code word for ugly. We hear women start-ing to describe the friend they want us to meet as having a great personality and we start running through our mental calendar looking for excuses why we just don't have any time this year to go out on a date.

The truth is this: If a relationship is going to last for a long time or even forever, most brothers want to give themselves the best chance at success. That means choosing a woman who is going to keep our attention riveted at home. If she's not attractive, that's going to make every woman who walks past our line of sight during the day look all that much better. Sure, we need to have willpower and resist temptation and keep it in our pants and yadda, yadda, yadda, but if we're being truthful with ourselves, men know that having the best-looking mate that you can manage increases your power to keep it in your pants. We may have to look at this woman for the rest of our lives. We want the view to be as inspiring and enjoyable as possible.

If appearance isn't the most important attribute to a woman looking for a man, isn't it pretty close to the top of the list?

From a Sistah

Sure it is—but we're not going to avoid all human contact with him just because he doesn't look like Denzel. We sistahs are much more forgiving—way more open to the idea that we need to adjust our standards in the looks department if we're going to get a man. We understand a bit better that looks mean nothing when it comes to finding a viable mate.

Granted, it takes us a bit of time to get there; we come from the same society that puts all too much stock in the shape of a woman's breast, the length of her leg, the color of her eyes and hair, the thinness of her nose, the thickness of her lips, the shade of her skin. We beat ourselves up if we don't fit the standard beauty types. *Nobody* can be more cruel than a woman evaluating the looks of another woman. I can assuredly admit to snapping on another woman's dress, or the way she had her hair fixed that day, or her inability to get her makeup to do what it's supposed to do. And then I'll say to myself, "Self? God doesn't like ugly," and I'll remember that my girlfriend Chrisena Coleman wrote in her brilliant pregnancy book, *Mama Knows Best,* that an old wives' tale for expectant mothers warns that you shouldn't make fun of unattractive people, lest your child come out looking like them.

To some extent, we hold guys to that standard. I talked a lot in *The Sistahs' Rules* about our need to use our hearts and not our eyes—to make sure that we're not simply passing up good men because of the way their face looks or the way their belly hangs or how firm their arm muscles are. We do tend, sometimes, to paint our picture of the ideal mate into a "square box" image that strangely resembles heartthrob celebrities.

But that's for the weak and shallow—and a lot of us sistahs have long ago forsaken those outdated standards for more realistic ones. We can (eventually) get over the fact that you're a bit over-weight if you're sweet to us. We can (eventually) get over the fact that you're shorter than we like if you're honest and true. We can (eventually) get over the fact that your left eye twitches for no reason in particular and that the knot in the back of your head is permanent if you've got some money, a job and enough sense to treat me right. We'll simply look into your right eye and remember to buy you a nice hat for Christmas.

That's to say that when we grow up, we stop judging books by their cover. We learn to examine what's in the contents before we decide you're not a good one. Perhaps it has something to do with the perceived shortage of black men. You know the deal: Beggars can't be choosers—booger bears are welcome if they've got something to offer. Perhaps there's a measure of desperation here—but I'd like to think that we sistahs are just a bit more open-minded when it comes to matters of the heart.

But this mode of thinking, I assume, doesn't appear in the brothers' handbook on dating. You know what they say about assumptions, though. So how about it:

If a sistah has a nice personality and is generally a good person but she's not all that cute, does she have a chance?

From a Brother

She might have a chance to be a real good friend, but we're not going to be trying to marry Miss Nice Personality. A nice personality is just not enough, for the reasons I explained above. When Miss Nice Personality is in a bad mood, what would we be left with? We can't even tell her she looks cute when she's mad.

It's our prerogative to make appearance an important attribute, just as it's yours to decide not to date drug addicts. The world will pat you on the back and say no one has to enter a relationship with a dude with serious jaw-dropping baggage if they don't want to—then the world (of women) will spin around and hiss evilly at us for strolling past Miss Nice Personality and asking Miss Fly Girl to dance. I realize Miss Nice Personality didn't have any control over the goods she was given. She might even have figured out a way to maximize what she has to make herself even more attractive than anyone ever thought she'd be. If so, she should be applauded for her effort. But why do I have to go out with her?

Remember that old adage: There's someone for everyone. If that is at all close to the truth, then I'm not upsetting the world's rotational spin by deciding Miss Nice Personality isn't cute enough to be my soulmate. If soulmate means perfect match, wouldn't looks be a crucial part of the match? You wouldn't want two personalities that are as compatible as water and oil to give it a go, right? So why the different standard for physical appearance?

Of course, as I said before, if the brother has a view of his own physical attributes that is detached from reality, the sistahs will be quick to let him know about it when he steps to them— unless he has the other qualities they're looking for in enough abundance to overcompensate. Sistahs aren't shy about giving the flat hand to any brother who has made a misstep. We kinda expect that from sistahs. Why should brothers be saddled with the burden of picking a plain or "not all that cute" sistah? Can't we look to the fly girl, just as we'd pause to watch a breathtaking sunset?

As I will discuss later, personal style is an important part of the equation for us. If a Plain Jane carried herself like she's the flyest creature on earth, she's going to make us stop and take notice. We're going to suspect that that sistah-girl must really have it going on to feel the way she does about herself and not be afraid to let the world see it. That confident, sexy stroll, the head held high and proud, the easy, knowing smile, the self-assured laugh—when put together properly, these attributes can be almost as effective as a pretty face in luring our attention.

Impressions: What Makes You Want My Digits?

From a Sistah

Went to D.C. to visit a friend of ours, and just as Nick and I were climbing out of the car, we noticed three guys walking down the street toward us. Nothing unusual. Saw this woman with a short-sleeved shirt and a pair of cute jean shorts and platform shoes walking away from us on the same sidewalk. Nothing unusual. Saw the three men revert to little boy status, damn near breaking their necks to check out the lady's form as she passed—turned their bodies fully around and began walking backward and giggling and slapping each other on the back and quietly telling each other how sexy she was. Unfortunately, nothing unusual.

Frankly, we sistahs don't understand why the sight of a pretty girl with a nice figure (hell, half the time she doesn't even have to be cute; she could just be showing a little leg or a little bosom, or shoot, just be a woman) causes men to just act all stupid and stuff—like they've never seen female body parts. We say to our-selves, Surely there must be more to it than this—the operative "it" being the connection that we broker to make you think you want to talk to us and get to know us better.

And in some cases, that is true.

We recognize that some guys are just like dogs chasing after the bone—literally. We also recognize that most guys aren't so damn obvious about it—that he might actually want to feel us out before he makes the first call, and that he might actually want to go out on a date with us before he gets to begging us to, well, you know. It is those guys that we haven't a clue how to respond to.

Like, when we go out to the club, or we're on the subway, or we're in the bookstore, and you've noticed us and kicked up a conversation, we don't quite know how to handle it—haven't a clue what to say or how to conduct ourselves in order to get you to want to keep talking to us. We've been taught from birth to let the guy make all the first moves—but after that tidbit of advice, we're pretty much lost from there. Oh, some of us have some skills—can keep up a good conversation and make him laugh and give off the impression that we'd be a lot of fun to be around. But that's just some of us.

The rest of us just front. We laugh a little harder at your jokes, we sip our wine seductively or stare extra-hard into that book in the same section as you, act like we're actually interested in what you have to say. And we wait . . . And then we wonder to our-selves, "Dang, was I staring too hard? Was I talking too fast? Was I talking too loud? Did I walk away too fast? Did I not walk away fast enough? Did my girls turn him off? Was there lipstick on my teeth? A booger in my nose? Damn, is he going to come back over here?''

You all set the tone, and we follow along. If we like you and you're interested, most of us are going to wait for you to display that interest before we move on to the next step in that love connection. We're not going to ask for your digits, or tell you we should go out; we're going to wait for you to say it. And if you don't, well, we figure you weren't interested because if you were, you would have asked.

So we wait for the cues, silently wishing all along that we knew what it was that we should do to get you to talk to us some more and, perhaps, ask us out on a date.

What initial impression does a woman have to make in order to get a brother to keep talking to her and perhaps ask her out on a date?

From a Brother

When brothers are in the company of a new sistah, there's a quick but certain checklist that we fly through. These are the initial impressions that will decide whether we will even try to get to the talking stage. Once we have made our move and decided to talk with the hope of talking leading to more, she's already passed through the bulk of this list.

I present here the Brotherman First Impressions Checklist:

1. Face
2. Butt

3. Breasts
4. Legs
5. Personality
6. Personal Style
7. Clothes

Of course, the face is what we notice right away. There are many things brothers will say about a woman's body and her various body parts, but the grille (face) definitely belongs at the top of the list. The face is not going to change a whole lot over the years. It's going to remain fairly permanent through childbirth, through weight gain, through weight loss, through bad haircuts, through bad hair days. This is one of the God-given attributes that the woman and her future partner must live with forevermore. Our reaction to the face depends on several factors that have more to do with us than with the woman. If she's particularly beautiful, among our first thoughts will be the question of whether we possibly have any chance of getting play. In our experience, the Halle Berrys are likely not going to be sending us big-time "come hither" vibes, so we're probably going to be on our own in determining whether we should approach. Many of us ultimately decide just to stare from afar and never take that step. The ones with a better record of success in these situations might give it a shot.

Butt, breasts and legs can be interchangeable, depending on the particular brother. I put butt first because that happens to be my preference—and that of most of the brothers I encounter, as well as the body part most frequently mythologized in rap and hip-hop—but a healthy, dramatic pair of breasts or legs certainly won't fail to attract the black male eye. Whichever of these is your strongest suit should be played up, or kept in strong consideration when you shop for clothes or decide what to wear for those special occasions. This may sound like obvious advice, but I'm always shocked by how badly many women feel about their bodies and therefore are reluctant to play up their strongest suits even when trying to be noticed. They might even try to *hide* the prize, like a big butt, for instance. Imagine that. As if we want it hidden. As if it *can* be hidden.

Personality is of prime importance, but it has a hard way to go if it's going to overcome deficiencies in the other areas. A woman with very high points in the last three categories—personality, personal style and clothes—might come out all right in the final analysis, but the brother is going to need to be blown away if he won't have at least a pretty face, or perfect legs, or a big round booty to keep him happy and esthetically sated. We're talking Mother Teresa crossed with Oprah—and a little Vanessa Del Rio thrown in to give her some edge.

The Brotherhood needs at least two of the Big Four to get juiced up. The personality, personal style and clothes are big, but they're not enough to make us approach if everything else is shaky. In contrast, a pretty face and slammin' body will cause us to overlook low scores in the last three. We might figure that your cat might have just died (explaining an unpleasant personality), you're still young and unworldly (explaining the lack of personal style), and your apartment building just burned down (explaining the bad clothes—it also would explain the other two). These are things that can be improved upon over the years.

However, the Big Four (face, butt, breasts, legs) can't be altered—short of a visit to the plastic surgeon.

Women have determined for the rest of us that an enticing personality should be good enough for us to fall madly in love. And if we behave as if we want more, such as a pretty face or bodacious body, we are shallow and superficial. Were any men in the room when y'all voted on this one? It just doesn't jibe with the way men look at the world and look at women. I'm sure that there are plenty of guys out there who have chosen a mate based largely on a winning personality, but the overwhelming majority of us are going to try to do as best as we possibly can in the looks department. We're going to use all our visits to the mirror as a base, then we're going to look outward and see which women appear to be reasonably good matches. Then we're going to slide up to them and try not to insert our feet in our mouths. Sure, a nice personality is wonderful—and in fact it is what separates the women we wind up dating just a few times from the ones we fall in love with and want to have our children—but as far as early impressions go, it rarely can overcome zero face and zero body if the woman is going to make a lasting impression on us.

I'm not saying every woman we date has to be a beauty queen. We do sometimes go out with women whose looks leave something to be desired. But in the backs of our minds we're going to be second-guessing our choice unless she's so wonderful in every other way that she starts looking more and more attractive over time.

Both sexes appear to make similar calculations. Otherwise, if women didn't also consider a man's looks in a comparable way, there would be many more mismatched couples walking around in which the woman was far more attractive than the man. But most couples appear to be reasonably well matched, suggesting that women are looking very closely at face, in addition to all those other things they claim.

When the female gaze moves across the room and takes in a brother, what's she looking at—and looking for?

From a Sistah

Having his teeth helps. His looking at my face and not my ass— that's a plus. The first words "Yo," "baby," and "chocolate"—if those are avoided in his approach? Yep, his chances of holding a sistah's attention improve substantially. Clean fingernails and shoes that aren't run over, a breath mint, personality and a Visa card would buy you some time, too. Doesn't sound too difficult, does it?

Good, because it's not all that deep. We simply love beautiful black men—love the way they walk, the way they talk, the way they look, the way they smell, the way they make us feel protected and loved and sexy as all hell. Poet Nikki Giovanni, an absolute genius with words, put it perfectly in her poem "Beautiful Black Men" :

> i just wanta say something
> bout those beautiful beautiful beautiful outasight
> black men
> with they afros
> walking down the street
> is the same ol danger
> but a brand new pleasure

sitting on stoops, in bars, going to offices
running numbers, watching for their whores
preaching in churches, driving their hogs
walking their dogs, winking at me
in their fire red, lime green, burnt orange
royal blue tight tight pants that hug
what I like to hug

jerry butler, wilson pickett, the impressions
temptations, mighty mighty sly
don't have to do anything but walk
on stage
and i scream and stamp and shout
see new breed men in breed alls
dashiki suits with shirts that match
the lining that complements the ties
that smile at the sandals
where dirty toes peek at me
and i scream and stamp and shout
for more beautiful beautiful beautiful
black men with outasight afros.

Yeah—beautiful, beautiful, beautiful black men. Most of
them don't have outasight afros anymore, but they're outasight
just the same. We love the way you fit into those suits, the way
you step with your confident selves, the way you hold that bottle of beer and smile and laugh with your boys and cheer on
the game—the way you slap five when you talk that trash. We
adore you.

What are we looking for, you ask? A man. Not a boy, but a man, with strong hands and a strong heart and feelings and respect who knows a lady when he sees one—and sees her as a lady, for real, not just because she has boobs. What are we looking at, you ask? The sign. Not the one that tells us, "Idiot boy, stage left—run while you can!" We're looking for the one who tells us he might be a pleasant person to talk to over a candlelight dinner—someone who will treat us like a person and care about what we have to say and the way we react to what he has to say. We want a smile. We want a man who will ask active questions and inspire our minds. We want him to flirt. We're looking for the man who looks like he will be open to the possibility—the possibility that this doesn't have to end after just one night, that we can think about doing this and wanting this and loving every minute of this.

What do we want, you ask?

The possibility.

We're strong women, though—and we don't see too much point in going out of our way to get your attention. We don't want to play ourselves, or make it seem like we're easy or anything. Besides, why should I have to change my way to fit into your world?

Why should women be so concerned about impressing a man?

From a Brother

I know there are plenty of women out there who think this way, but it still confounds me. If you'd like to share your life with a man, then at some point it will become necessary for you to persuade a fellow that you are someone he would like to spend time with.

Simple, right? It's a concept that men understand almost too well—we'll make up stuff if we have to in order to ensure that the woman is impressed. But many women seem to operate with the belief that they will be selling out, or disgracing themselves, if they make even a tiny move that is intended to impress a man or get his attention. Love would be nice if it followed them home and knocked on their door, but if they ever turned their head or moved their eyes to actually look for it, they think they have diminished or cheapened themselves. This makes about as much sense to me as trying to save money by spending every dime you have.

We want you to be friendly to us. We want you to talk to us. We want you to act like you want us to talk to you. We don't want you to play hard to get, because it's a bore and it confuses the hell out of us.

But sistahs these days aren't trying to hear any of this.

A few years ago, I wouldn't even have believed these women were out there, arduously laboring to give men the impression that they don't need men and aren't looking for one. But on quite a few occasions I'd notice that one woman or another was particularly mean or dismissive in my presence and my wife would tell me it was because she liked me or was attracted to me. It defied logic, so at first I refused to believe this. That woman who sat next to me on the couch for an hour but never looked my way, never acknowledged my presence, who spoke to every person at the entire party except the one closest to her—she was attracted to me? Hell, if the situation were reversed, I'd certainly want the woman to know I existed if I expected anything to come of it. What would I get out of ignoring someone I was interested in?

As I watched women in different situations, I started noticing all the times when they ignored me or other men in instances where at least a greeting or a glance in my direction would be expected. Not that I'd want to run home with them, but perhaps I was the only brother in the room or the one closest to them and a conversation with an attractive sistah wouldn't be a bad way to pass the time. But I'd get no conversation, no acknowledgment, nothing. I started to feel like the sistahs were telling me something: "Don't expect me to talk to you or look at you or notice you because you're the only brother in the room or I'm attracted to you or I like the cut of your suit or I couldn't help but notice the way you walk while you weren't looking." It seems that many women go out of their way to feign disinterest so brothers won't get the mistaken impression that the sistah wants something from us. So we walk away wondering why the sistah was so evil and unfriendly, then we see her ten minutes later laughing at every utterance of some goofy guy in the corner. In this situation, the only message we're getting is that the sistah is whack. If something else was supposed to be communicated to us, it flew way over our heads.

I know many sistahs—and brothers, too—operate under the belief that men are more attracted to the women they consider aloof and unattainable. You know, that challenge thing. The game is the hunt and all that. There have been times when I also was into the hunting game. But you know what I discovered? Often-times, those very same qualities that drew you to her—the cool, distant, disinterested personality—become the very same qualities that drive you away from her once the two of you are trying to forge a relationship. How did that saying go? Be careful of what you ask for, 'cause you just might get it.

Why is it a sign of weakness for a sistah to want to give brothers the idea that she's interested and maybe even go out of her way to snag one? If the sistah has worked on all the inner strength stuff that Iyanla Vanzant and Susan Taylor and my wife talk about in their books, isn't she then ready to put her inner strength to work to get the things she wants? If those things in-clude a man, a love partner, an emotional assistant, can't she try to impress him the same way that she would a potential boss if she were trying to get a new job? If that means taking an earlier train in the morning to strike up a conversation with the cutie pie who lives around the corner, or finding different excuses every day to pass by the office of an attractive colleague, or pretending to be looking for oranges to rub elbows with the fine brother in the fruit aisle, why not? What's the harm? Is it wrong to want a man, to grow tired of that cold bed and takeout for one? Have we reached the depressing point where men are so despised and harmful that a woman has to pretend she isn't interested in us to gain the respect of other women in certain circles? It's okay to latch onto a best friend and let her run your life, but if you give any power or control over your emotions to a person with a penis you have sold out the gender? Doesn't this thinking have women putting on lipstick and makeup on the sly, telling anyone who asks that it's for themselves and other women that they want to look good—NOT for a dude? I hear this one all the time and it always makes me wonder: What's wrong with wanting to look good for a dude? Who wrote the rule book saying that was wrong? When these women step from the shower and look in the mirror, are they thinking: I hope my friend Natifah likes the firmness of my butt? I don't think so.

Brothers don't respond to coldness. First of all, we're not going to even know that the sistah who's been ignoring us at the cocktail party has actually noticed our presence, and we're certainly not going to take her disinterest as an invitation to approach. As a matter of fact, we're going to stay the hell away from her. A few of us may be intrigued and challenged and try to start up a conversation, but that's what she wants—a chance to prove to you that she's not interested. And if later on we find ourselves riding down on the elevator with her, even if we're forced into a conversation, in the backs of our minds we're going to suspect that she's one of those cold, hostile sistahs who thinks every black man is trying to get into her panties. My brother-in-law, James Eo, thinks it can sometimes be healthy for some egomaniacs to be brought down a few notches by these cold fish, but what about the other brothers—the ones with the manageable egos who just want a little play from a pretty girl? Knock them down a few notches and you have to bend over to talk to them.

Women should want to impress us—should want to be more friendly, warm and willing to strike up conversations—because that's what the sexes do, impress each other to assist in the mate selection process. It's what animals do and it's what humans are programmed to do from the time we set foot onto the playground

for our first kindergarten recess. When women start trying to sub-
vert this natural process and go out of their way NOT to impress
us, we're going to flee in confusion. These are the kinds of games
that mess us up, leave us scratching our heads and wondering what
in the world sistahs are thinking.

Playas

From a Sistah

See, it was cute in high school—this idea that you had to be on the arm of the most handsome, debonair, smooth guy in the joint. There were a few of them at Brentwood Ross High when I was there—Sean, Rudy, Kenyon, Keith, Matt, Parish. They had this reputation, you see. They were jocks, they were handsome, they were funny, they were, in some cases, smart, and, above all else, they were cool. And they'd stand out in the hallway, looking just as fine in their Lee jeans and their LeTigre shirts and their Kangols and their gazelles and their shell-top Adidas and name belts—just standing there, watching the folks go by, holding court in their clique up against the wall, laughing and joking and grabbing onto the arms of the girls they thought were cute and worthy of their attention.

And Lord, if I didn't want one of them to just reach out and grab my arm, too—to throw me some of that attention that people like the twins, Lori and Stacy, got, or some of the chicks on the cheerleading squad. Because you know if they grabbed up on your arm, then you were in there—the in crowd, a lady of the playa squad. You were invited into their special circle, assigned the privilege of going to their parties, riding in their (parents') cars, sitting with them at the lunch table, cheering for them on the sidelines of their sports games, wearing their name belts for the week.

I don't know that folks recognized themselves as "playas" back then—but clearly these guys had some juice and they weren't afraid to drink in the benefits of popularity, namely, getting down with the ladies. And who could blame them? They were high school boys, and high school boys will do just about anything to get some play— and if they happen to be fly or a jock or noticeably talented in any way, and little girls were going to swarm all over their bodies and give them some? Huh—you damn skippy they were going to take advantage. If that meant dating one girl one week and then next week moving on to the next honey and two weeks after that dropping her for another—well, they were going to do it. So long as there was a supply and they were in demand, it was on.

But that was high school.

You don't expect that kind of behavior to follow through into adulthood. But, unfortunately, it does—and with grown men who should know better. Watch them work it in a club; champagne flowing (or forties, as boing has absolutely nothing to do with class), they'll work a roomful of women like a newly released convict in a whorehouse. The pen flies across the inside of match books and corner pieces of napkins faster than a Coltrane riff, the phone numbers just piling up in their jackets and pants pockets.

And then they'll take them all home, spread them out on the bed or the table or whatever, and proceed to hold court on the phone with each one, setting up their little appointment books with dates that would even tire out the playa president, Bill Clinton.

Of course, it extends outside of the clubs; if there's a woman on the street, in the post office, at the car wash, on the train, at the job—shoot, just in their line of sight—guys seem to have no problem macking, just rolling up on a sistah and expecting before the conversation is through to have the home number, the work number, the fax number, the beeper number and a date. And before she can make it around the corner or out of the room—shoot, simply out of earshot—he's moved on to the next woman, running the same ole lines he just finished using on the last chick.

They can be five or fifty-five—doesn't matter—tall or short, rich or dirt funky poor, in the restaurant alone or alone while his girlfriend is in the bathroom—all of them are playing. Shoot, at least in high school, you understood why the cute ones were always macking; they had every right to—the girls loved them because they were handsome and popular. But today he can be broke with one leg and a kickstand, and as long as he has a penis, he's got license to just play, play, play with women.

It's like it's a game—a childish, immature, stupid game—and we sistahs have almost no other choice but to participate in it if we want some male companionship. It's stick and move, stick and move, stick and move. Most of us sistahs think it's a dick thing. But perhaps you can help us out:

Why do brothers insist on dating eight billion women at the same time?

From a Brother

All brothers want to be seen as playas, particularly by other brothers. But eventually we grow out of it. It just takes some of us longer to get to eventually than it does others.

It might sound silly from the outside, but while we're struggling through adolescence, the most honored, significant talent a male can have is an ease with the ladies. This grants you entry into any social clique you desire—nerds, jocks, preppies, druggies, they all think you're the coolest creature on the planet. Other males watch in awe as you saunter up to the prettiest girls in school and calmly engage them in actual conversation and maybe even get a—gasp!—laugh or smile to spread across their faces. And if you are able to turn that ease into sexual conquests—or the appearance of sexual conquests—the other males in the school are ready to hang a plaque in your honor on the wall. Just like with everything else, that's where the playa mystique all starts: high school. Sistahs may nurture their envy of the girl with the bomb body or the one with long hair; brothers gaze jealously at the mack daddy.

This thinking has been exaggerated one hundredfold with the rise of the hip-hop nation. These days, if they're not bragging about their cars or their toughness, rappers are crooning about how many "hoes" they've "hit." We've moved from Superfly, Shaft and The Mack to Biggie, LL Cool J, and Uncle Luke. But the idea is still the same: all cootchie, all the time. When sixty-plus-year-old Hollywood legend Warren Beatty desperately wanted to hang around rappers to research his film *Bulworth,* it was his infamy as a playa that moved the rappers to allow entry to the aging white man.

This all is not to say that all brothers forever endorse the playa lifestyle. Most of us grow up, get jobs, get tired of the dating/singles scene, meet a special woman, and decide to become a one-woman playa. We see that sharing the love of one woman is ultimately far more satisfying than sharing a bed with the Freak of the Week. Sure, this sistah might have a bigger booty, or that one might have a better technique, but in the end it all winds up becoming the mechanical act of sex without emotion. It all starts feeling the same.

We all come to this realization eventually; it just takes some of us longer to get to eventually than it does others. Some may view these men as immature. I don't think that's necessarily the case. They're just finding it harder to make up their minds.

Men are also plagued by the wandering eye, the grass-is-greener trap. Some of us need to put in quite a few years of living before we can get it out of our heads that the grass isn't necessarily greener across the street in that red dress—it may look greener from far away, but once you get up on it you realize it's the same thing you got at home: grass. In other words, we need to look around a little bit and see what's out there before we can truly appreciate a special woman when she walks into our lives. Making this discovery about the grass is definitely a function of growth, of maturity. We all get there eventually—it just takes some of us a hell of a long time.

I know some of the females out there don't always want to wait that long—I can understand that. Waiting can be a bitch, particularly if you aren't absolutely sure the brother is worth it.

At the risk of toppling the Brotherhood, I suggest to sistahs that if your wait started when Bill Clinton was still scratching his ass in the governor's mansion in Little Rock, you've been waiting too long.

But not all women are looking to get married every time they meet a new brother. Some girls just want to have fun.

If that's the case, who better than a playa to rock your fun-loving world?

From a Sistah

I'm a huge proponent of women thinking more like men when it comes to dating. We spend entirely too much time trying to make the one standing in front of us "The One," instead of going slow, dating a healthy multitude of men and taking the pick of the litter. The latter, I guess, would qualify us as "playas"—but there would be something strangely more liberating and fair about our approach.

The chief difference here would be that we wouldn't be focused on the actual chase. When guys get around some women, (it seems) they're talking to every skirt in the room not because they're looking for "The One," but because they're looking for "The One Tonight." I never got the impression that those little black books are filled with numbers because homeboy is on a strategic search for a wife.

Chances are that if a sistah were to take the "playa" approach by dating three different guys at the same time, she'd do it as part of an honest search for a mate—a lifetime partner—and she'd size them up against one another, considering which one is the guy most likely to make her happiest. She'd more than likely be more honest about it, too—letting each one of the guys know that he's not the only one, that she's still mingling. And she'd more than likely let each one of them know that she's looking to settle down eventually—and that if he plays his cards right, she might expect him to be the one.

And oh, she wouldn't be sleeping with all three, either, a concept that guys just don't seem to really grasp when they're dating more than one woman.

Basically, there'd be a fundamental difference in the style of play—one that just wouldn't be complementary to a brother's style of play. That means that even if we did choose to play the field—and, I'm sorry to say, we don't enough—a brother playa would just mess up our game. No sistah likes a playa. We may be enamored by him for a quick minute, may give him a lil' somethin' here and there, may be thoroughly charmed by his advances—but the moment we smell something fishy in the air, the moment we suspect there might be some other heffa on his agenda, most of us are going to step. Granted, there are a few sistahs who would stick around and play, for fear that the brother in front of them is the only game in town, but the less gullible of us aren't going to have it—and we shouldn't be expected to. We don't, after all, expect you guys to put up with that kind of behavior; it's a respect thang.

Answer us sistahs this: **How would you feel if you were one of the guys on the list of a female playa?**

From a Brother

Are we talking female playa of the brother variety—that is, dating and sleeping with a wide variety of men—or one of these bogus halfass playas whom you described above who supposedly is sizing up three different men at the same time but not sleeping with any of them? 'Cause I don't really call that virginal, curious sistah a playa—she's just a sistah who can't make a decision. But if you're talking about a sistah who's out there collecting phone numbers and doing her share of pole-vaulting, a freaky Nola Darling–type Mack Momma who's just gotta have it and will tell you in a heartbeat that No, she's not available on Friday, Saturday or Sunday, thank you, because she's, uh, busy—well, she'd confuse the hell out of me and make me feel bad.

A female playa wouldn't be a problem if sex was the only thing we wanted from her. We might even be excited by the idea because we'd have some pretty high expectations, based on our perception that she's been around the world a few times. This female playa would stay on our minds because of her blatant sexuality, but wouldn't get an engagement ring from us unless one of those asteroids in *Deep Impact* had leveled every other female on the planet. And even then, we'd start feeling insecure when she stared at the surviving horses a little too long.

Because not many of us have any experience with this female playa, we'd have a hard time figuring her out. This isn't to imply that we feel capable of actually figuring out any specimens of the female species, but we feel comfortable categorizing the women we meet into "types," just as author Van Whitfield did in his novel *Beeperless Remote.* The female playa is not one of the types our catalogue of experiences can instruct us on associating with. She's just not in the Brotherhood Manual. Many of us would be tempted to label her "ho," and expect her to eventually hold out her hand looking for our loot in exchange for the booty. But once that didn't happen, most of us would be stumped. We'd wonder what she was after—why was she giving it up to so many dudes if she didn't want anything? I don't think it'd ever cross our minds that she wanted just sex—even though that's clearly the case for so many of us. The catalogue tells us that this isn't one of the programs in the female hard drive—wanting to be with a lot of men just to have sex with them. I'm sure she's out there, spreading her love and her legs, but when we run into her, we're looking for some other motivating factor besides sex.

Using sex to find a husband just would not work, which I suspect is why you conveniently removed that aspect from the equation in describing your female playa above. Once we got wind of her past, we'd have such a hard time with the memory of other male hands clutching those buns that we'd be forever suspicious, waking up in the middle of the night and wondering what other Negro is on her mind as she hugs her pillow so tightly.

I shouldn't say that getting the ring is impossible, though. I have a friend who gladly married his girlfriend even after she boldly threw in his face evidence of her very recent communions with other penises. First, she invited an ex-boyfriend to stay with them for the weekend. As the woman showed her ex to the door at the end of the weekend, my boy was in the garage looking for a hammer to hang a picture. When he walked back toward the apartment, he glanced out of the garage and what did he see? His woman leaned back over her ex's car, giving her ex some major tongue as her arms wrapped around his neck. When my boy yelled out to them, she didn't rush toward him tearfully and apologize profusely, as most of us in the Brotherhood would have expected.

No, my girl hopped into the car with her ex and they sped off. And it doesn't end there. On another occasion, he came home early and caught her on the phone with a different guy, telling the dude what she would do with his piece if he were there with her. I think they call that phone sex. But that still wasn't enough to stop old boy from presenting this freak mama with a ring. It's been a few years. The marriage is still a marriage. Maybe by now homegirl has learned to do all her phone sexing at the office.

Yes, a female playa presents us with a major challenge. She'd be giving us a taste of our own medicine and all that. We'd hate it. Yeah, it's a double standard, but we don't like tasting our own medicine. We want to be the doctor, not the patient. And as for this fake female playa my wife has hypothesized who is seeing three different men but not sleeping with them, that wouldn't work, either—we wouldn't believe her if we found out about the other dudes. We'd ask ourselves, what would be the point of her balancing these dudes if she wasn't getting any? That's not something we'd do. We might keep one woman around for a while if we really liked her, but we're not going to bother balancing three women in three platonic relationships. That would be like cheating on a test with a crib sheet on which you only list half the answers. All the risks with none of the benefits. You get caught and tell the teacher, "But, um, I only had half the answers." What's the point in that?

The Digits: What Makes You Call Again?

From a Sistah

We saw each other at the bar, we had a great conversation, I gave you my number and said, "Call me sometime." You did, and we stayed on the phone for hours—talked about everything under the sun. The conversation got so good we were one step from the scene in *The Truth About Cats and Dogs,* the one where the main characters get to know each other during an all-night chat session, in which they talk and giggle and make tuna fish sandwiches and read to each other and play music for one another, and, finally, get it on together—all over the phone.

The date? It was just as sweet. Great dinner, great conversation, great evening stroll. This is a date to remember. And you drop me off, ever the gentleman, at my front stoop, and tell me you'll talk to me soon.

And I wait.

And I wait some more.

And I sit by the phone—and, you guessed it, I wait a few minutes more.

I pick up the receiver, make sure AT&T hasn't shut my joint down, tell my girl to call me back just to make sure the ringer isn't broken, and then, assured that absolutely nothing is wrong with my phone, I hang that bad boy up, put my chin into my palm, and wonder what the hell I did wrong after what I thought was such a wonderful date for you to *not* use the digits again.

I mean, you said you would call. A week later, nothing. Two weeks later, still nothing. A month later, I've pretty much surmised that you weren't interested.

There isn't a woman on this earth who doesn't want to know the answer to this question:

Why do guys say they're going to call, and then don't?

From a Brother

There's no vast conspiracy going on. We didn't all get together in the men's room and decide not to call y'all back. There are probably as many reasons for the lack of a call as there are men who leave you hanging, but if I were forced to generalize, I would say this: We don't call because we don't wanna talk to you.

The reasons for that could be quite complicated. Some of us might think the sistah is out of our league. Some of us might think the sistah doesn't quite approach our league. Some of us might have waited a little too long, and then we were embarrassed after three weeks. Some of us might have thought you didn't really like us. But if I were a betting man, the reason I'd put my money on is that brothers don't call because they aren't quite available and able to start a relationship with somebody else.

Call it a corollary of the grass-is-always-greener way of thinking: We see something we might like, we try it out to see whether it's better than what we already got. We're not sure if our present woman is our Forever Soulmate. So we continue to look around to see if she's still out there. No, that does not mean we're playas who creep around, trying to have sex with as many women as we can. It means we're still looking for "The One" because we're not sure whether we already have her.

If we discover the one we took out on that date is not "The One"—or that it would take too much effort to determine whether she is or not—we go back to what we already got.

So when we take you out on the date and you figure a great time was had by all, perhaps the reason your phone isn't ringing is because the brother has decided he'd better stay with what he already has. This could mean you're not pretty enough, or smart enough, or sexy enough, or ambitious enough, for him to trade in his present girlfriend, but it could mean none of these things. It might just mean that it would take too much emotional effort to start a new relationship—he doesn't have the stomach to go through a breakup scene at the moment. He also doesn't have the stomach to readapt to a brand-new woman.

If, however, several months go by and you get a phone call from the brother out of the blue, it probably means that for whatever reasons, he just wasn't getting along with his woman anymore.

I'm not trying to imply here that men are always on the lookout for newer models to trade in for—we're not that cold and shallow with our love lives. But before we reach the stage where we consider ourselves ready for marriage vows, we are looking around to see what else is out there. We think of this as part of our learning curve—the only way you can find out what you really want is to sample everything available to you. A few feelings may get hurt in the process, but that's probably preferable to us falling into a long-term commitment and then coming to the conclusion somewhere down the line that we made a mistake and we're trapped.

If the man hasn't called, there's also the other possibility: He didn't have as much fun as you did. I think this may happen more often than women realize. When women aren't enjoying themselves on a date, they're not hard to read—teeth-sucking, deep sighs, and disinterested conversation are clues we have no trouble figuring out. But when a man isn't having a good time or doesn't think she's the one, the last thing he's going to do is tell the woman this because that would ruin any chances he might have of getting her panties off. We'll suffer through so-so conversation and a complete lack of chemistry or spark if we think there's a chance the woman is giving up booty. With a new woman, we don't know if she's the sex-on-the-first-date type. So we smile nicely, respond warmly to her questions, open up her door, pay for her meal, even tell her we had or are having a nice time. All in the hope that we might wind up getting some.

By the way, calling a woman isn't always the easiest thing in the world for us. It puts a major premium on having something interesting to say. We know that we're usually the ones expected to start the conversation, and to keep the conversation moving along, and to eventually get to the purpose of the call, so sometimes we have to psych ourselves up before we call. Maybe even have the conversation scripted out. (Okay, now I'm frontin'. If any guy out there has actually scripted out a phone conversation, he should be shot and put out of his pathetic misery.) So we have to be totally ready to make the call before we pick up that phone. For some of us, it might take more than a few days before we get to that point. I'm not saying this is a common occurrence, but I'm sure it happens.

While we're on the subject, how come you can't call us?

From a Sistah

We have been conditioned from birth to let you do the work.

You know what I'm talking about—don't you? While Dad was telling his son to respect the little girls from around the way—and then silently winking and nodding and slapping his son on the back talkin' 'bout "you're a little playa after my own heart, son"—Papa was telling his little girl to "Leave them lil' boys alone."

We were warned to wear dresses that fell respectably past the knee, cross our legs, never talk up or out of turn and be ladies at all times.

And if he revealed himself to be a gentleman, we could give him our number—but, Mommy and Daddy warned, "Don't you ever—ever, ever, ever—call him first."

"Nice girls don't pick; they get picked," they warned.

And that's just the old-fashioned baggage we carry.

These days, that's coupled with the fact that we can't stand rejection and will do everything within our power to walk away from the situation without looking like a complete idiot. The last thing we sistahs want is for a brother to think we're chasing his behind, because you know what happens when a brother knows some woman is sniffing his tail.

He'll run off in the other direction.

We're afraid that if we pick up the receiver and dial his digits, he'll get on the phone like, "Oh, hi. Um, I'm a little busy—can you call back in, like, the year 2010?" Then he'll go off with his boys somewhere, proudly proclaiming that some biddy he met at the club "keeps blowin' up my spot, man."

"She won't leave me alone," he'll say with a sly grin.

And we will look like complete, stone-cold idiots—or at least think we do.

I don't necessarily agree with this concept. As I wrote in *The Sistahs' Rules,* a sistah needs to go on ahead and get over it and call that man—since he's as scared of rejection as we are, and would probably be completely turned on by the fact that she got over her inhibitions and dialed the digits.

But this rule was, perhaps, one of the ones that a host of sistahs said they just couldn't get their hands around. Too used to letting him do the work.

That means that if the couple exchanged phone numbers at the club and he said he was going to call, we're expecting him to do just that: call. We'll also be expecting him to ask us out on the date, make the plans, and pay for it all, to boot.

"The mouse should chase the cheese," one sistah told me.

"That's just the way I was brought up," said another.

If he doesn't call, well, then, we figure he wasn't interested, anyway.

Eventually we get out of this and go on ahead and call the brother. But not until we're sure that we're not getting played in the process. In the meantime:

What can we do to make sure that after that initial hookup, you'll call again?

From a Brother

About the only thing you can do to make sure we will call again is to be yourselves.

This question really comes down to what can the woman do to make sure the man likes her. No one has that much divine wisdom. There are things to make us more likely NOT to call, but there's no way to predict whether a man and a woman are going to hit it off. If a woman is too nosy, if she's too pushy, if she's too loud, if she's too tacky, if she's too dumb, if she's too fat, if she's too uncouth, if she's too tall, if she's too intense, if she's too nervous, if she's too vain—these are some of the reasons we don't call again. If she's none of these things, it's hard to say what she needs to do. But there's something that will help increase the odds that the brother will call again—be nice.

As I've said before, we like to be around nice women. And if a woman is fine AND nice? Ohmygoodness, we start shopping for an engagement ring. Because men have gotten it into their heads that *fine* and *nice* don't often go together. We think pretty women have been so pampered and spoiled—and also so harassed and oft-propositioned—that they no longer even know how to be sweet and cordial and caring to men, if they ever knew how in the first place. These assumptions—okay, these stereotypes—may be off base in some cases, but the fact remains that a pretty woman has to prove her niceness with us before we'd believe it. In other words, we assume bitchiness until she proves otherwise.

If being warm and friendly is a stretch for you, don't wait by the phone.

Work It: What Should We Do to Achieve the Perfect Date?

From a Sistah

We've all done it.

You know, leave work two hours early to give yourself time to prepare for that first date. You fall up into your bedroom and tear it to pieces, looking for the perfect outfit to slide into, the perfect makeup to spread across your face—the perfect 'do. The upsweep? The fall? The red pumps? The black sandals?

And then—straight out of a bad blind date movie—you assault the mirror with your Mack Mama poses.

"Hello," you say, a little bass in your voice for that sultry sound, hands gently sweeping the mirror frame for emphasis. "Nope. Too fast."

"Hello," you say again, a little higher—for the cheerleader rah-rah thing. "Nope. Entirely too cute."

"Hi," you say, waving. "Uh-uh—no, you didn't. Entirely too corny."

You hit the profile. You hit the dead-on. You tilt the chin. You check out the booty—hike the skirt up an inch.

Then you sit by the door and wait for him or climb into the car to get to him, pop Altoids, constantly check the mirror for boogers and shake and sweat and mumble to yourself all the way to your destination—scared to death.

The source of the anxiety?

We are anxious to dazzle. We want to dazzle him because even though we would never admit this to a brother's face, we ALWAYS have lurking in the back of our minds the possibility—the possibility that this might lead to another date, and then another date, and then another, and then that love thang, and then that marriage thang, and baby thang—that together forever thang.

And the possibility of any of that happening is basically dead and stinking on contact if we don't work it right on the first date—or so we think.

But once we get past the nice shoes, the auto 'do, the clean nose, the fresh breath, it's pretty hard to figure out how we go about achieving that perfect date—the one that will get us invited back for another. **So help us out: In the male mind, what is the perfect date?**

From a Brother

Damn. Can I be real stupid and obvious and say, one that ends up with our bellies bumpin'? That's not working for you? All rightie, then.

I think it comes down to talking.

Many brothers out there might initially balk at that one—I can just hear it now: "What?! Talking? This brother is whack!" But listen up.

I've never been able to figure out why, but I know for sure that I just have an easier time talking to some people. Maybe it's pheromones or brain waves or common experiences—whatever it is, there are times when you stumble across a person with whom you just seem to vibe. It could be a member of the opposite sex or same sex, a cousin or co-worker, a bank teller or a first date. When it happens, you sense it right away because you feel like you've known the person your entire life and there's no dark secret or private thought that you wouldn't be willing to share with them.

The perfect date is when you and she finally hit a pause in the conversation, you look up at the sky, and you are both stunned to discover that the sun is rising and you have just spent six hours talking. You couldn't even effectively summarize everything you talked about because the conversation had a life of its own, charging ahead with no plan, no grand schematic. You just talked; and you laughed; maybe you even cried. And it was easy; and it was maybe the most fun you've ever had without your privates getting wet; and you never want it to stop. It's like being zapped by a lightning bolt and living to talk about it—you know that something special and rare has just happened and perhaps your life will never be the same.

These are the kinds of encounters that can't be forced or planned—they just seem to happen without warning, like a force of nature. But there are things that both parties can do to nurture an environment where the lightning might be more likely to strike in your direction:

1. Be yourself. Don't try too hard to impress the other person. It's brilliantly clear that when you get zapped on that perfect date, you are responding to what is real and touchable in the other person, not some bogus facade erected to impress.

2. Don't try to be too coy or cute. We can detect this right away. Those women who are playing the game of being mysterious or who are laughing at all of our jokes—even the ones that aren't intended to be jokes—can be ID'd and labeled from a mile away. You're about as subtle as an elephant. And after awhile we're thinking you're either a fake bitch or dumb as hell.

3. Ask us questions, but don't push us too much into revelations. If we want to tell you, we will. We don't respond well to pushy women—we imagine what she'll be like a year down the line and we feel like running in terror. Talk about yourself—if we like what we hear and see, then you won't be able to shut us up. When it's going perfectly, we find ourselves telling you more than you'd ever think of asking anyway.

4. Vibe-ing isn't the same as arguing. While many brothers—such as myself—like women they consider intellectually stimulating, we aren't usually looking for a debate partner. If the woman looks like she is the type to treat the relationship like a mock trial, we're not bound to be too eager to come back for round two. That means that those contrarians out there who can't help but disagree with every statement they've ever heard— shut up! Listen without judging for once. Talk without arguing. And if you are truly a contrarian extraordinaire, you're not likely to achieve the status of perfect date partner unless the brother has a serious jones for masochism.

5. We're not really looking for sex right away—we're always looking for sex, but the kind of woman who would come close to perfect date status probably ain't giving it up right away, so we would like some clue that you find us physically attractive. That means it's okay to flirt in between heartfelt outpourings—you know, engaging smiles, lowered eyelashes, seductive body language. The works.

But after all is said and done, could this male standard for a perfect date ever pass muster with the womenfolk—or does your idea of a perfect date require us to sign over at least half our paycheck and reveal our plans for marriage and children?

From a Sistah

Actually, Mr. Smart Butt, those of us sistahs who are not gold diggers and have our own paychecks don't particularly care about how much you brothers spend on our date. In fact, we independent-and-loving-it sistahs might be more inclined to offer to split the check—pay our own way—rather than let you spend your little money on us.

That doesn't mean that we don't need a man to do anything for us; it simply means that we don't like it when a man flaunts his wealth in our face, then makes us feel like we somehow owe him something for taking us out. It may sound like a cliché, but some brothers are still mentally dividing up the menu into "Budget = I'm Not Getting Any Play from This One" and "Expensive = I'm Getting Some Tonight"—and then going out of their way to make us feel guilty if we're not giving up the booty.

Then there're the brothers who think they're impressing somebody by flaunting their wealth in our face—telling us about the Mercedes and the mansion and his partner status and dropping names and acting like we're supposed to be impressed by it all.

Can I get a witness? Hello!

Well, quite the contrary to what you think, gentlemen, we couldn't give a rat's booty about you sitting there and telling us how much money you make or the kind of car you drive or the titles you have or the people you know—because we sistahs who truly know how to play the game already knew that 4–1–1 before you slid into the chair.

Can I get another witness? Hello!

We don't want your résumé while we're sipping our wine. We want the same thing you want—a smooth conversation that'll not only be interesting, but will put us at ease. We don't want to have to sit there and pretend to laugh at your jokes, pretend to be interested in what you've got to say, pretend to be having a good time. We want to laugh for real, we want to be interested in what you have to say, we want to have a good time. And we want to go home after having had that good time without being accosted or being made to feel guilty because we don't want to wake up in the same bed with you the next morning.

Our dream date is steeped in respectful companionship.

Yes, it would be nice if you spent big money on us—yes, it would be nice if you picked us up in the gleaming white ride and swept us off our feet with all the materialistic things Cinderella got from the prince at the ball.

But it's not the only thing we want—and, in the end if we're really sincere about finding The One, it's nowhere near the top of the list anyway.

We simply want you.

Can I get a witness? Hello!

Whose responsibility is it, anyway, to lift a date to perfect status, mine or yours?

From a Brother
The responsibility is shared equally.

She has to be an engaging partner, but the man also has to do and say all the right things at just the right moments. But he can't do these things as part of a preconceived plan because then it's phony and forced. To be perfect, most of the night must be spontaneous and unforced. It must flow as easily as a freshwater stream. Natural. That's the word of the day. You can't assign roles and responsibility with natural. It's either natural or it isn't.

I remember a first date with a woman who was trying much too hard. I could almost see the veins bulging in her forehead from the effort to laugh on cue whenever she thought I was making a funny, or to smile whenever she felt that I was about to look in her direction. By the end of the dinner, *I* was exhausted from the hard work she put in. This woman was assuming too much of the responsibility of trying to make it work. If she had just sat back and let the feeling flow, let the real her emerge from beneath the artifice, things would have gone much better. I went out with her a few more times (the sistah *was* fine), but after the third date or so I kinda lost her number. I was worn out from watching her strain.

Baggage

From a Sistah

Had a sistah turn up at one of my book signings for *The Sistahs' Rules* with this compelling statement: "Brothers are always trying to hide shit."

And she just shut the room down with that one.

Said she was tired of going out on dates with brothers and getting hot and heavy into relationships and finding out that he conveniently forgot to tell her that he's got two babies by two different women and the babies' mommas' taking him to court to stick him for *all* his papers and that he ain't working, he livin' with his daddy (temporarily, he insists) and, oh, he got, like, two, three honeys he's dating right now this minute—one of them his ex-wife—even though he made it seem like it was, "Just you and me, babe."

Girlfriend said that she always lays out her stuff on the table—always lets her potential mates know if she's dating, if she's involved, what her grand relationship plans are, that she has a daughter and the child's father is very active in her child's life.

"I just lay it all out there," she said, "because he deserves to know."

I think a lot of us sistahs are like that. We're just so much better at talking and displaying emotions and, frankly, being honest. We want him to know what's up because we don't want to waste anybody's time. If he's turned off by any of the aforementioned luggage we're towing, then he's free to step *before* we get into a serious relationship and he decides he can't deal. Better he leave now rather than wait until we get used to his behind than he leave because we held back something he should have known from the beginning.

It just feels better to us to be honest.

Somehow, though, this sentiment doesn't necessarily get translated into the way brothers deal with relationships. **Why do you guys hold back on information about yourselves when you're starting a relationship with someone?**

From a Brother

Eventually, we all collect a certain amount of baggage. I'm sure there are things that even these sistahs who are being so honest and open on the first date hold back until later so as not to send the brother running off into the night. I think men hold back the things we believe will halt the relationship in its tracks before it even becomes a relationship.

We tell ourselves that we'll give her a chance to get to know us first before we bias her against us with negativity. If she likes us after she gets to know who we are, she won't care about the two children. At least, that's what we're thinking.

There is a fundamental difference here in the way brothers and sistahs approach the early stages of a relationship. We want to see if the thing has any potential on its own before saddling it with things that are going to make the sistah frown. Sistahs throw it all out there from the start to test whether the brother is still going to stick around—or at least they claim to throw it all out there. Take, for instance, the matter of children.

If the sistah has a child or children who live with her, then she's right to tell the brother up front because those kids are necessarily going to become a big part of the relationship. Eventually he's going to have to meet the kids and maybe one day even become a father figure to them. If he's not ready for that, it's probably right for him to know up front.

If a brother has a child or children who aren't living with him, he probably doesn't think this is a piece of information he needs to throw out there on the first date. He figures he'll tell her in good time, but he doesn't want to poison her first. Because there are a long set of assumptions on the part of black women that come to mind instantly when they find out a man has a child: irresponsibility, carelessness, baby–mother ghetto drama, his pockets being siphoned (maybe—if he's paying any child support). These assumptions will be a lot harder for him to disprove if the sistah starts the thing off looking at him with this harshly critical eye than if she evaluates him without her eyes being poisoned first.

Brothers are just trying to give themselves the best possible chance with the sistah.

Sure, it looks pretty bad if the sistah finds out about the kids on her own or months into the relationship, after she has grown quite fond of the brother. We can't let things go on too long without revealing critical info. That's the error many brothers make. Rather than taking a deep breath and coming forward with it on the second or third date, brothers keep waiting, almost as if they were trying to hide it. And that's what it looks like: They were hiding it.

There are other kinds of troubles that are even more understandable for us not to reveal right away—prison record, drug addiction, rape convictions, alcoholism, child abuse. These are the kinds of marks on our record that could send a woman running off into the night before we even get our entrees. We really want to give ourselves a chance before we come forward with these, particularly if the things happened in the distant past and have little to do with the man we've become today. If I've had a substance abuse problem and have been clean for five years, is it wrong for me to wait a few months before telling you that? How realistic is it for me to expect a woman to want a second date if I tell her on the first date that I still count the number of days that I've been clean? This is a mighty big mental hurdle for her to jump in the beginning. Perhaps she'd eventually be able to get beyond it, but my guess is she's not going to want to try. So I wait, thinking if I do it any other way I may never find a partner. Sistahs may say this is wrong; I say it's practical.

My friend Shawn Dove describes the early dates as the brother "trying to make the sale."

"He's only going to extol the virtues of the product," said Shawn, ever the salesman. "He's not going to emphasize the draw-backs."

Sistahs need to be honest about this.

Even if I've been clean for years, how eager are you going to be for a second date if I tell you on the first date that I'm a recovering drug addict?

From a Sistah

There would be no second date—but it's my right to make that call before I get into a serious relationship with you.

I know this is precisely why a recovering drug addict wouldn't tell a person like me that he used to be one with a crack pipe, but you know what? If I'm dating you and can reasonably assume that a few more dates could lead to a long-term relationship, I have the right to know with whom I'm dealing.

We sistahs want you to put the cards on the table and let us decide if we want to play. True, everyone wants to put their best body forward when they're getting to know someone, but keeping back vital information makes it too easy for people to end up getting hurt when the truth finally reveals itself.

Take, for instance, my girlfriend's friend Fran. Fran started dating Will, whom everybody in town except Fran knew had been gay for a good forty of the forty-five years he'd spent on this earth. At some point, though, Will got into the church and decided that his homosexual lifestyle was against God's law, and so he went on and switched over to dating women. Which was fine, except that he couldn't quite suppress his sexual needs for men—which Fran, of course, was not.

So while he had Fran believing she was dating—and having unprotected sex with—a heterosexual man, Will was skipping around town making the *acquaintance* of others. Some of her girlfriends finally let her in on Will's escapades, and when she confronted him about it, he 'fessed up. And as you can imagine, all kinds of things were going through Fran's mind—Do I have AIDS? Am I not a good enough woman? How could he do this to me?

The drama was enough for E. Lynn Harris to fill several bestselling books.

Her heart was shattered—as was her trust in men. She had the right to know up front that he was bisexual, because that information could have been vital in her deciding if she wanted to run screaming in the other direction, or if she wanted to date him but protect herself and expect that he could decide he wanted another man over her.

You liken holding back information to extolling the "virtues of the product" and "trying to make the sale." Well, if you walked into what you thought was a reputable department store, and a salesman proceeded to talk you into purchasing a thirty-six-inch television he swore was the top of the line and "brand spanking new, lady—I promise you," and then you got that bad boy home and it broke down and when you took it to the shop you found out that it was a used TV made in 1990, not 1998, like the salesman led you to believe, you wouldn't like that, would you?

Well, we sistahs don't like to be lied to, and we damn sure

don't like surprises, unless it comes wrapped in a nice little box and glistens when we open the package.

You have a drug condition?

Let me know.

You're dating four or five other women?

Let me know.

You have some type of infectious disease?

Tell me something.

You used to/still are sleeping with other men?

You best come clean.

But since you guys obviously don't feel the same way, how much should a woman reveal about herself when she first begins to date you?

From a Brother

Wait, before I answer the question, let me get this straight: You're telling me brotherman was supposed to pick an entree, hand his menu back to the waiter, lean toward Miss "Fran" and tell her, "By the way, dear, I like penis"? I don't think so. The problem there was not that he didn't come forward and tell her he used to hit from the other side of the plate—the problem was that he was running around cheating on her.

The fact that the cheating was going on with other men made for sensational headlines, but it was the cheating that got him in the news in the first place. What if he never again touched another man? Is she still supposed to know right away about the former men in his life?

This question is a tough one. Except for knowing whether the woman has bedded down the New York Knicks' starting five, broth-

ers probably aren't quite as interested in a woman's past as sistahs are sweating ours. We're much more focused on the present. In some cases, we probably should do a little bit more investigation— perhaps brotherman should be more curious about why his woman turns red and throws things at him every time he drives up Tenth Avenue and makes fun of the "hoes" doing the stroll. But we presume that we can tell most of what we need to know about a woman by spending a little time with her. Sometimes we're right; sometimes we're not.

I guess brothers need to practice what we preach. If women think we're being evil and duplicitous by not immediately revealing all the sour notes we've hit over the years, then I suppose we shouldn't expect to find out everything about sistah-girl right away, either. Once again, I still believe that sistahs only tell us the bad things they believe we're going to soon find out about anyway. For instance, how likely is a sistah to tell us on the first date that she was sexually abused as a child and still hasn't quite gotten over her sexual hang-ups? That's certainly going to become a major issue in the relationship, but it's not the type of thing women usually go around advertising.

Sometimes even knowing about our past doesn't help. There was a well-publicized case in New Jersey in which a man met his second wife during his trial for the murder of his first wife. How did the second marriage end? He killed her, too. Now that's what I call a man with some serious baggage.

White Girls

From a Sistah

These sistahs had gone down to the Black Expo to do a little shopping—but if they could check out some brothers while they were there, they were definitely going to do that, too. So there they were, standing around this Coca-Cola booth, getting free soda to quench the thirst they'd worked up, when he walked in: A Hershey's special dark chocolate Adonis—tall, fine, body beautiful from head to toe.

There was barely a woman at the Coca-Cola booth who wasn't either looking at him or trying to make his acquaintance. He smiled at his admirers, and even exchanged pleasantries. But he only had eyes for one woman—and when she came skipping in behind him, all mouths dropped.

For she was a blonde, blue-eyed white girl.

That's right, sistahs, a white girl.

And she walked right on up to him, planted a sweet, juicy kiss on his lips, took his hand and led him on off into the caverns of the Expo site.

Conversation ceased. That corner of the convention center came to a complete standstill. You could have heard a roach relieving himself on cotton—that's how quiet the sistahs got.

He had clearly committed a serious sistah-girl violation.

I have no doubt that those who witnessed it were saying the same thing my girlfriends and I were: "Damn! There goes another one."

Sure, he could have been in love with the girl—she could have been a perfectly lovely, sweet, intelligent person whom he simply enjoyed being around. And yes, in this day and age, we don't need to be all up in the mix of a man we don't know, trying to tell him who he can and cannot date.

But this one fact remains: Any brother who shows up to the ball with someone who looks like the original Cinderella is gonna get called out by the sistahs—or at least talked about after the party's over. And that goes for every sistah, from the one who's physically repulsed by the sight of a white girl wrapped around a brother to those of us who are down with the "Color Doesn't Matter Committee." No matter how repressed or progressive we are when it comes to matters of the heart, we all think the same thing when we see her and him together: Either brotherman has that self-hating identity complex thing happening, or he thinks black girls are somehow inferior to Cindy.

I was once on a television panel discussing this very subject, and two brothers showed up talking about how they prefer white women because the black women they'd dated just weren't good enough. And they said it with conviction, too, like they'd made a conscious decision to get a better job, a better car, a better house and oh, by the way, "let me get a white girl to go with this lifestyle upgrade because, you know, we need the finer things in life."

It may not be that complicated for him. But all he has to do is show up with her—doesn't have to say a word—and almost every sistah in the room will think about that logic for a fleeting moment, some way more than others.

Can you blame us?

Every time we look at the television screen, some African-American male celebrity—whether a sports professional, model, singer, whatever—is hugged up with a white woman. I have a girlfriend who is married to a professional football player, and she's downright traumatized by the fact that after the game, when she waits in the back of the stadium for her husband with the other NFL wives, she is one of the few—and I mean very few—sistah-wives in a sea of white ones. I should add that her hubby's team is about 98 percent black.

And celebrities aren't the only ones. There are parts of the country where you can go for days without seeing a black man with a black woman. According to the latest census statistics, the fastest-growing segment of interracial marriages is that of black men to women who are not black. Of the 350,000 black-white marriages in the U.S., 70 percent are unions of black men and white women—a statistic that shows that black men are more willing to cross over than their female counterparts. The numbers are still incredibly low—those same statistics point out that over 98 percent of married African-American men are wedded to black women—but perception is everything, regardless of the stats. It's getting to the point now where we secretly applaud brothers who actually give a black girl some play.

And we hurt.

Tell us: Why do brothers have to be the CEOs of the Rainbow Coalition—forsaking the sistahs for white girls?

From a Brother

It's hard, real hard, to defend the brothers on this one, let me tell you. My heart's just not in it. But I'll try anyway.

We've all seen and heard the sistahs react upon sighting a brother with a white girl—the neck roll, the teeth suck, the hip jut. Spike Lee tapped into this with the free-flowing condemnation during his sistah-girl round table in *Jungle Fever*. Their responses are predictable and vehement—and let's face it, brothers have given them many years of practice. Still, many brothers continue to go there. They take the step knowing what their sistah friends will say, what their sisters will say, what their mothers will say. You can step out with a Latina, a Chinese woman, a lady from India, even a man—none will garner the attention of a white girl.

What is the lure? That's the question a lot of sistahs throw out. Surely it's not an easy one for brothers to answer. What we frequently hear is, "I fell in love with a woman, not a white woman." And who can jump up into a brother's head and know what he is thinking and wishing, what his motivations are, when he pursues a relationship with a white woman? I certainly can't. But when we put all the second-guessing aside, there are some hard-hitting things we can say with certainty.

One, the anger of black women makes perfect sense. The much-discussed shortage of eligible black males has become almost a truism in our community and society at large. What with the prison population, the drug addiction rate, the unemployment rate, we have been told over and over that a huge chunk of the black male population is out of commission. Some of this is surely exaggeration, but there are undoubtedly elements of truth mixed in there. All one need do is ride through our communities in the middle of an afternoon to see that many of us aren't up to a whole lot besides standing around—and harassing the sisters on their way to and from work. So if *shortage* is too strong a word, we can probably admit to an imbalance between available black women and available black men. Therefore, every brother who steps out with a white girl is one fewer brother available to a black girl. It's simple mathematics, and sistahs transform themselves into walking calculators when they see one of us go there.

Two, there's enough baggage littering the history of black-white relations in this country that the motivations of black men can definitely be questioned. White women have been held up as the unattainable, unreachable, inaccessible, pedestal-perching model of female pulchritude throughout our stay in this country. Since our days in bondage, she has been the untouchable. And considering the way the human mind functions, there's probably no better way to make something desirable than to declare it unattainable. So when a brother does seek out white women, it is entirely possible that his quest is a human reaction to history. If he parades around with a white woman, he is both announcing that he has achieved something that had been unachievable and is also exacting a certain revenge. This could be conscious or not.

Black women know this, black men know this, white people know this. Some of this could even be going on when white women desire black men. There's so much history and baggage lurking beneath the surface here. Who's to know whose motives are entirely pure?

Like a lot of black men, I always knew that if I went there, I'd have some extremely uncomfortable moments after I brought her home to Mom and Dad. Don't misunderstand me—Mom wouldn't spit in the girl's face or toss arsenic in her food. She'd be reasonably charming and pleasant because that's her nature. And Dad would be his usual courteous self, asking all the right questions and making just enough teasing jokes at my expense to make her feel like my family was perhaps opening up to her. But, oh, just wait until Mom got me on the phone the next day!

I'm imagining all this because I've never brought home a white girl to meet my parents, not even after spending four years around them every day in college. Certainly there were some I found attractive and engaging and friendly, but something always held me back—just as I sensed that many of them also had little voices in their heads holding them back. I suspect my voices were those of my mother, my sisters, my aunts and female cousins and generations of black women, living and dead, who have forced it into their little boys' heads over the decades that they are not to be bringing home any girls who couldn't use an Afro comb.

I know plenty of brothers whose thoughts are as Afrocentric as mine and the rest of the black male community, yet they go home to white girls. Just as a brother wouldn't ask another brother why his woman is mean, or fat, or lazy, or overly flirtatious, or why she drools on herself, black male protocol dictates that you don't ask a brother why he's with a white woman. That's considered a matter of the heart and conscience, off-limits to the public. Sure, we all wonder, and some of us may talk about him behind his back—okay, most of us—but it's rare for the brother to have to explain that kind of decision to us. Though I am troubled by the seeming spate of interracial couplings among successful black men, I think it's healthy that brothers are given the freedom to make their own choices without hearing the world's condemnation. These brothers are going to feel and see the anger enough anyway, so there's probably no need to voice it, too. We should all be given the right to live our lives as free as our consciences and our sense of decency will allow—as long as we aren't breaking any laws or causing anyone harm. Brothers have had their movements and choices so severely restricted throughout this country's timeline that there would be something tragic and wrong about our own community rising up to step into a man's bedroom. Yeah, it'd be great if one day every black man woke up and discovered the beauty of his own women and vowed that he had to go out and get one for himself, but that's unrealistic. There are so many factors that go into a brother choosing a woman, and if she's white—well, maybe he just liked her. It doesn't have to be all motherland-deep.

What we all need to do is realize that we are a strong, beautiful, desirable people who don't need daily affirmation from the outside world or from our community to truly feel that. If we could pull that off, we wouldn't care what O.J. brings home with him next week.

The fact that 98 percent of us are gladly deciding to spend the rest of our lives with sistahs isn't enough to make you feel

beautiful and wanted and needed? Isn't your anger kinda like looking at a glass that's filled almost to the brim and angrily exclaiming that you can't drink from the glass because it isn't completely full?

From a Sistah

Yes, we do understand that there is a huge number of brothers out there who are committed to their sistahs as lovers, girlfriends and wives— but despite the paltry numbers, the incidents lean far too heavily on the side of prominent, successful black men to be dismissed as mere coincidence.

I could cite them for days—from O.J. to James Earl Jones, Quincy Jones to Clarence Thomas, Sidney Poitier to Charles Barkley. Go down to Wall Street, and see how many high-powered brothers down there are courting white women. It's not hard to figure out the message here—that white women are somehow better. And there's a double whammy because these are our knights in shining armor, our black princes. If they are going elsewhere, that substantially reduces the number of black Cinderellas out there being swept away to the glistening mansion on the hill.

It also means that these very high-profile men who are in the public eye—on television, in the newspaper and the like—are constantly seen with their hands interlocked with white women's, and sistahs are rarely to be found anywhere on the radar screen. It simply seems that all too often, when black men achieve a measure of success, they grab for a white woman.

Everyone from writer Eldridge Cleaver (*Soul on Ice*) to Spike Lee (*Jungle Fever*) has explored our feelings on the subject. And singer Me'Shell Ndege Ocello put the perfect voice to our frustration when she sang in her 1993 song "Soul On Ice" that black men who seek out "virginal white beauties" are rejecting "motherland brownskin."

"You want blond hair, blue-eyed soul/slow white passion without the hot comb," she purrs. *"Take a look in the mirror—you don't love yourself. Your soul's on ice."*

Those comments—a shared sentiment by a lot of sistahs—are steeped in pain, and it doesn't matter how paltry the numbers are, we ache for each and every one of you. The fact still remains that there are brothers dating white women.

You don't need to make a long leap at all to see how an interracial coupling can be seen as a rejection of us sistahs. The image of the white beauty as perfect woman is used to sell everything from cars to soap, projected from billboards to movie screens. If we don't look anything like her, does that mean we are far from perfect, far from beautiful? It's hard day in and day out not to think so, particularly when even among us, the more a black woman looks like the white beauty, the more beautiful she is deemed (no disrespect to our fair-skinned sistahs; y'all know what we're talking about here).

These are issues we sistahs deal with every day. When we look in the mirror, we must ignore the messages that bounce off our brains on a daily basis, and find other sources besides our mamas and *Essence* magazine to tell us that we are beautiful. That's not easy. One of the sources we look to, though, is our men. But if they're too busy confirming the larger society's view of beauty— or even strutting it in our faces by dating white women—that is bound to make us just a little disagreeable.

Don't you all think the same way as we do when you see a sistah with a white guy?

From a Brother

The sight of a sistah with a white man raises our eyebrows and a lot of questions, but if there is any anger in our reaction, it is a very nuanced anger.

We may wonder what she sees in him, but we wouldn't dare confront her or toss a wayward comment in her direction for fear that she might turn around and angrily ask why we didn't care when she was walking alone or with a black man who treated her worse than a stray pet. A part of us may abstractly believe that we all need to stay together, and we may want to remind her of the sordid history that the two of them share throughout this nation's nasty past. But we don't feel qualified to tell all that to sistah girl, who may have spent the last thirty-five years waiting for a Brother Mr. Right who still had yet to materialize.

The sight doesn't slap us with the same kind of rejection that many black women feel when they see us sliding down the white slopes. The sight of a sistah with a white man doesn't touch us in deep, hidden places the way it seems to touch black women the other way around. We just don't feel that our beauty or sexuality or desirability is challenged on a regular basis by mainstream society, so a sistah choosing a white guy isn't something that we take personally.

We have questions, yes. But anger? No.

Gimme the Loot: Am I a Gold Digger Because I Want My Man to Be Paid?

From a Sistah

Why lie?

It may sound harsh—but hey: A huge amount of us who are beautiful, hardworking, independent sistahs figure that if we're bringing a certain amount of stock to the table, our man best be sitting down to our Wedgwood with stock, too.

Who can blame us?

We grow up sistahs in this capitalist society, we study long, work hard, and those good grades turn into good jobs turn into fabulous careers turn into decent/sweet salaries? We pretty much figure that any man stepping into our world best come correct or stay his behind at home. That doesn't mean that the only man we'll date or wed is one whose bank account rivals that of Bill Gates; it simply means that he has enough money to combine with ours to take care of us, family and home.

Of course, if we're making money ourselves, we don't need a man to handle our financial affairs; we're self-sufficient—quite capable of handling the rent, the bills, the car note and the kids on our own. Nobody—and I mean nobody—on this earth is better than a sistah at making a dollar out of a dime and a nickel, and miraculously using it to make some ends meet.

But that doesn't take away from the fact that some of us think a man who plans on making our acquaintance has to be self-sufficient, too—and, in some of our minds, able to not only buy the bacon, but the eggs, toast and fresh-squeezed orange juice, too (shoot—wouldn't mind if he could fry it up in the pan and never forget I'm a *wo*man, either!). The simple fact is that while we can take care of ourselves—and do—it's always good to know that when we need to depend on someone to pay the bills and put food on the table and keep some loot in the bank while we take off from work to have kids or we lose our jobs or we simply need a break, we can depend on our man to handle that business.

It's what we've *all* been conditioned from birth to expect.

Still, the moment a woman brings up the fact that she's expecting her lifelong partner to have a couple dollars in his pocket, the sistah is called out, deemed the lowest of the low: a gold digger. Brothers get to throwing pickaxes and shovels and hard hats at girlfriend and swirling accusations through the air, forcing them to land on us like daggers in our backs. "Man, all these women want to do is get in my pocket," they say, and, "Look out, all she wants you to do is take care of her kids," they charge.

To them, she is nothing more than a high-priced ho in a business suit.

And we think that's unfair.

Granted, there are some sistahs out there who make it hard for those of us sistahs who are on the up-and-up. They slide up into that hootch gear, wrap their fingers around an expensive bottle of champagne (paid for, of course, by some fool who didn't know any better) and zero in for the kill. All they want to know about you is two things: Are you paid and is you buying. They may throw you a little some, a few times if you're lucky. And then, all of a sudden, you're sending her expensive gifts and paying for expensive vacations and losing your natural-born mind. And then you slip up, she catches you out there—and you're stuck with a living reminder that there is a woman out there who gamed you lovely and has made it her life's mission to suck your pocket bone-freakin'-dry.

And then I come along and innocently ask you what you do for a living, and you run in the opposite direction like a plum fool, like I done stole from your mama and your firstborn.

We sistahs are bothered by this. Those of us who are not gold diggers—who are simply concerned about our welfare, well-being and future—clearly know the difference between a woman who wants a good life and a woman who's using men to live the good life. You brothers, though, don't seem to distinguish between the two. **So tell us: Why are we sistahs tagged as gold diggers just because we'd like our men to be paid?**

From a Brother

Yeah, the name is harsh, and the sentiment behind it isn't kind, but let's not front: We all know they're out there. Most of y'all have at least a few friends whom you describe in this way behind their backs or to their face when they get you pissed. Some women are more obvious about it; hanging out at the players' entrance to the stadium is a symptom of obviousness. But others try to do it on the sly, the down-low.

Most men have stumbled upon both the sly and the obvious varieties in our day, even if we don't have a lot of money (we get trampled as they run us over to get to the brother with loot). We start developing a sensor that we feel is just as reliable as the one women think they can use to spot gay men. Not only does our sensor give off a screaming beep inside our heads, it also comes equipped with a locking device that instantly seals our wallets inside a pocket vault. That way, we can feel more comfortable if we're actually caught on a date or in the clutches of one.

I'm not trying to imply that there's anything wrong with women hoping to connect with a man who is financially stable, or even rich. That's their prerogative. But gold diggers approach it with the zeal of big game hunters. For them, the numbers in the bank account are of the utmost importance, elevated above what's in the head or the heart. They think happiness comes in the form of the Mercedes S class or a fully loaded Land Cruiser.

For those men whose sensors are rusty or women who aren't sure if you or the women around you register on the gold digger scale, I present here my own tips for discerning whether a woman is a gold digger. If you are a man and you find yourself nodding in agreement with too many of these descriptions, as if I followed around your current woman with a video camera in order to write this, perhaps you should start working on the prenup right now. If you're a woman and you are sporting a blush in full flower when you finish, I have one word . . . ho (and that's not a half-assed Santa imitation).

You know she's a golddigger if . . .

• She can look at the material and cut of your suit and tell you which salesman at Barneys sold it to you.

• When she shook your hand for the first time, she looked at your watch instead of your face.

• When she found out you are a professional basketball player, she opened her bag and pulled out her NBA salary chart—which she'd had laminated.

• When she found out you are a lawyer, she opened her bag and pulled out her *Martindale Hubbell* lawyer directory—in which she'd developed her own rating system for the law firms.

• She tries to order lobster at IHOP.

• She has the local sports teams' schedules memorized so she always knows exactly how many professional athletes are in town.

• At the club, she won't dance with you until she sees a résumé.

• When she spotted your college ring, you could have sworn you heard a moan escape from her lips.

• She buys *Fortune* magazine for the pictures.

• In her apartment, you spotted a voodoo doll that looked remarkably like Camille Cosby—with a pin stuck between its eyes.

• Her bed has a cash register next to it.

• She subscribes to Street and Smith's high school basketball scouting magazine—she says you can never start too early.

• She buys *Black Enterprise* for the pictures.

• In her bedroom, she has a collection of engagement rings—all given to her before her previous fiancés wised up.

• She majored in recreational therapy to be near the football team.

• Instead of foreplay, she tells you to just keep repeating your annual salary.

• She won't talk to you if your car is older than the milk in her refrigerator.

• Her best friends gave her a pickax and shovel as a gag Christmas gift.

• The guys at the club instinctively check for their wallets after she walks in.

• Her car comes equipped with a siren and flashing lights that she uses to pull over every brother she sees driving an expensive car.

• Instead of shaking your hand, she extends her hand with her palm up.

• At the jewelry store, the stool that sits in front of the biggest diamond has her butt indentations in the cushion from her daily pilgrimage.

• When she shakes a man's hand and feels the hardened callouses of a blue-collar worker, she runs away shrieking.

• She goes to sleep in the fetal position, wrapped around your wallet.

Meanwhile, are women more willing to tolerate pain and heartache from a man who has money?

From a Sistah

He can be buck-toothed, cross-eyed and hobbling on one leg and a kickstand; to some of us, as long as he's got money, he's cool and the gang. Might even start to look cute, too. But it takes a special kind of somebody—let me rephrase: a screwed-up individual—to put up with a man's crap just because he can make up for it later with a nice gift or a fancy dinner. Not all of us fall into this category.

But Lord, if there aren't some of us who do. All one needs to do is to peruse the newspapers and television news broadcasts to understand how much crap some women married to money put up with. There're the celebrities and sports figures who cavort with other women and show their behinds in drunken public tirades and get fiercely physical with their women behind closed doors—all to the complete embarrassment and heartache of their significant others. And still, they stay.

Then there're the sistahs who date men who have absolutely no intention of committing to them, much less marrying them, yet they still let him into the house if he arrives to the door with some kind of fancy trinket and an excuse for why she hasn't seen or heard from him in two months. All is forgiven when she opens that little box. And still, they stay.

It's easy for us to assume that the reason why these sistahs don't book up is because of the money. To some extent, we're probably right. Because if he was a broken-down Will Smith look-alike whom she hadn't seen or heard from in two days, foot would have immediately connected to butt and he'd have been gone, gone—gone.

But we've seen women, too, who've dated, loved, married and had their hearts broken by that broken-down Will Smith and stayed with him anyway. Shoot—how many women have you heard of who've had their jaws broken by some man who didn't have a pot to piss in, only to show up in court the next day to beg the judge to dismiss the charges and let her man come on back home to her?

See, it totally depends on the woman—her strengths and vulnerabilities, her desires and her needs. For some, money solves it all. For others, a cute face or serious skills in the bed does the trick. And there are sistahs who won't put up with any of the aforementioned crap and would rather be by themselves than to be used by someone just because he has a few dollars in his pocket or a cute face or anything else.

One never knows which one he'll get.

So, enough about our fetishes with men with money. Are men attracted to women with money the way women are attracted to men with loot?

From a Brother

Only the laziest, slimiest, triflingest brothers among us would consciously go after a sistah because she has loot. That's just not the way most of us think.

We may chase a woman for some superficial or trivial reasons, but loot normally isn't one of them. Brothers who engage in this kind of big game hunting get absolutely no props from the rest of the Brotherhood.

We derive too much of our sense of self-worth from not only how much we have but how we got it. If you had to mack a female in order to get paid, your stuff is way too weak for words. If any of the brothers around you ever found out that was your game, you'd get so soundly ridiculed and chastised that you'd regret to your dying day the moment you revealed your plans. You might even get labeled with that harshest of nicknames: Steadman, in reference to the longtime beau of Miss Winfrey. Sure, Steadman has his own thing going on and he did before he hooked up with her royal TV highness, but that doesn't change the world's perception that he's just along for the ride. When my wife started to find some success after the publication of her first book, *The Sistahs' Rules,* a few of my homies jokingly called me Steadman a few times. They didn't mean much harm by it, but it just hammered home for me the discomfort that men AND women—hell, all of society—feel with the idea that a man is gaming a woman for her loot.

This doesn't mean that you become ashamed of taking advantage of your woman's good fortune if a Brink's truck just happens to dump its contents in her garage. If she works hard for the money and it starts flowing her way, you give her a big hug and congratulate her on her well-earned success. But you do not, repeat, you don't, make designs on her cash and decide that your love for her (cash) has just become undying. That's lame.

There may be something of a double standard at work here: we all probably are more tolerant of women who make the possession of loot a major requirement for their future mate. We think women should rightly be concerned about their security and a man's ability to provide for the family. But dudes aren't supposed to be looking to the female to do the providing. That's the way we're raised to think, the way societal messages condition us to look at the world. To break away from that view means incurring a great deal of wrath from those around you and the suspicions of every woman with at least a coupla zeros before the decimal in her banking account.

Of course, most black men are also fighting against a destructive stereotype that many of us are playas in search of a sistah to support us. The fear that sistahs will suspect us of being one of these lazy-ass playas motivates us to behave in as un-playa-like a fashion as we can possibly manage. This likely means bending over too far in the other direction to prove to the professional woman with cash that we got plenty of our own. This may even mean buying things we can't afford or blithely throwing around our rent money to exude the aura of a man with major bank.

I can honestly say that I'm still somewhat uncomfortable when my wife pays for something for the both of us with money that she earned on her own. A creeping embarrassment threatens to overtake me; I have to use every ounce of self-control to not say something ridiculous to her that will cause a major disturbance— something like, "Nah, baby, don't pay for dinner tonight. I got this—no problem. I'll just run down to the bank and take out a small loan to cover it." I know that these feelings are part of the baggage that being a black man in America has loaded onto my shoulders: that ever-present, vague worry about what people— even my wife—will think, whether they'll start wondering if I'm the same as the brother on the eleven o'clock news. A part of me knows that my identity, my sense of self, should have no connection to that brother on the evening news or that image of the playa just trying to run a game—I should know that as long as I continue to do the right thing by my family and my community, I don't need to prove to anyone what I am not. But it gets hard sometimes. Real hard.

Getting the Love
You Need

STOP! In the Name of Love: What's Wrong with Taking It Slow?

From a Sistah

Okay, so we'll let you in on a little secret: We really do think about sex as much as you men do. We simply think it's just a bit crass to talk about it in public 24-7–365—unless we're (a) with our girlfriends, (b) staring at the bottom of a tequila bottle or (c) all of the above.

In the instance of "c," it's our favorite topic.

We love talking about the times we, ooh—how the last one worked it out so lovely he had us "howlin' at the moon, chile," and how the one before him made us forget our name, or was so bad, he made us want to forget his. We tell each other when we last got some, how long it's been since we seen one, and our plots and plans on where we're going to get it, who's going to give it to us next, and who we'd just love to give it to.

Sex is not, however, something most of us want to talk about with a brother we've only dated two, three times.

Still, the prospect of it coming up sometime between when we sit down for our first meal together and, say, the time we take the last sip of our after-dinner drink looms entirely too large. From the time we say yes to your offer to take us out on our first date, we're wondering what tactic you're going to take to try and talk us into the sack. There's the ole, "Babe, come on—I just want to come up to your apartment to talk, really." And then there's the standard: "Aw, girl, come on—it don't mean nothin'. We're adults. We just gonna have a good time—no strings attached." And please, don't get me started on the Mars Blackmon approach: "Yes—I will respect you in the morning. Please, baby, please baby, please, baby, baby, please."

Oh it can get ugly, all right.

Granted, it doesn't get as obvious as that—most of the time. But it's an unspoken pressure; we're thinking that you're thinking you're trying to see the panties before the evening is over—even though you never said so. It's on our minds when we're slipping into our outfits, on our minds when we're arriving to our date destination, on our minds when we part from you, on our minds when we're waiting for you to call back—on our minds during each successive date until we actually commence to knocking the boots.

We can't kiss you without wondering if you're going to want tongue. We can't give you a hug without recognizing that the consequence might be that you'll want to touch a few other places while we're embracing. We know cuddling is out because that's certainly the universal brother signal for, "Aw yeah—it's on."

And oh my goodness, the anguish we go through trying to determine whether our decision not to have sex with you means we're going to lose you—and, even more importantly, whether our consenting to sex with you means that you've gotten what you wanted and now you're out, ghost, hasta la vista, baby.

In a perfect sistah's world, absolutely none of this would be an issue. We'd go out on a date with a dude and, if we liked him, we'd go out with him again—and the pressure of deciding when it's appropriate to have sex with him and trying to do it within a reasonable time (read: before he decides you're frigid and leaves your ass) would not be an issue. He'd want to get to know us better—explore our minds and our souls, contemplate a strong relationship before he got around to wanting some booty. There would be no rush.

But we all know whose world this is.

So tell us: **What's wrong with taking the nice, slow route to the sheets?**

From a Brother

We'll go fast, slow, medium—whatever is necessary for us to get into the panties. If a sistah wants to give it up right away, brothers aren't going to shake their heads and say they want to wait. But if a sistah wants to take her time before giving up the goods, the brother isn't going to run in the other direction if he really likes her. That last part is the key: our reaction is wholly dependent on how we feel about her potential as a partner.

If sistahs are under the impression that we will like them more the longer they hold out, they need to be reeducated. Not getting the booty doesn't make us like someone more. Not getting the booty just makes us wonder how long we're going to have to wait to get the booty. How much we vibe with a sistah, the ease with which we converse, the little chill down the spine that we get from the twinkle in her eye, the deep yearning we feel every time we get a whiff of her fragrance—those are all the things that affect how long we're going to stick around. Waiting for the booty is just what it says: we're waiting to have sex. If we like her, the sex will become an intoxicating part of our growing affection for her. If we don't like the woman a whole lot, we still may stick around to have sex, especially if she's fine and the booty has been talking to us. But once we hit the booty, we're not suddenly going to fall in love if that potential wasn't there all along.

In other words, the sex and the potential for a long-lasting bond are two entirely separate matters. True, the sex goes far to enhance that bond. But the sex certainly can't replace that bond. Many women may find themselves in strange relationships with brothers who seem to want only the sex, but aren't interested in sharing any quality time, like eating at fancy restaurants, late-night strolls in the park together, hours-long phone conversations. These are probably clear-cut cases where the brother is getting the booty but doesn't want the other stuff. As long as she keeps on giving it up, he's going to keep coming around. If she takes the step of telling him she needs a more serious relationship, homeboy will be sure to lose the phone number.

Men are easily able to separate sex from love. We'll tolerate all kinds of half-assed, broke-down "associations" with seriously damaged women if they're going to keep opening their legs like a drawbridge whenever we call. And you can be sure the calls will come late at night when there's no possibility that we'll have to commit to anything as scary as an actual date in public with the woman. This can go on for years, with the brother coming around whenever he gets horny and possibly sharing the same setup with several women at the same time. But once he meets "the one," the real deal, the whole enchilada, he'll forget those late-night receptacles without a second thought. The lesson? If those women thought that he was going to fall in love with them at some point because they were sleeping with him, they're painfully deluding themselves.

On the other hand, if that whole enchilada, that real deal, decides that she's going to make him sweat a little while before she gives it up—say she makes him wait three months or so—he's going to be following her around like a drooling puppy until she succumbs. He's not going to sprint in the other direction because she's keeping her legs closed. He's going to wait and hope the stuff is as good as everything else about her. (Granted, if she takes too long he's going to keep calling those late-night receptacles for a bit of relief, but he'll be back up in her face the next day, waiting and yearning and smiling like a pig in slop.)

Taking it slow isn't some kind of disease that we think will kill us. But we're always going to be anxious to get to the panties. We have complete confidence in our ability to have sex with a woman and still respect her as an honorable woman if we thought she was an honorable woman from the start, remain interested in her if she's an interesting person, and stay in the relationship if it's somewhere we want to stay. So we therefore don't see the need to make us wait. (After all: "We're both adults, baby.") Now, if we didn't think the woman was honorable, if we didn't think she was interesting, if we weren't keen on having a relationship with her in the first place, then hell no, we're not going to be rushing home to meet her mommy and daddy just because she gave us some poontang.

So, just as you want to know about our childhood and our family and our educational background and our salary and a million and one other things before you decide whether things are going to get serious, wouldn't you also want to know if we had any idea how to satisfy you in the sack? Wouldn't that just be another piece of your research assignment—to assess whether there was any sexual chemistry between us?

From a Sistah
Our deciding whether we want to stick with you is not wholly dependent on your performance in the sack.

It may be *one* of the deciding factors, but it's not going to be *the* thing that will make or break your future with us.

There's so much more that we take into account when we pronounce, "He's the one—my Brother Mr. Right." We're testing you on the regular—minute by minute—turning each and every one of your actions onto its belly, hoping that they bear out this one truth: You're the one. We want to know if the flowers you sent are a sign that you're sweet or you're trying to get over, whether your showing up late to our date means you're disinterested in the relationship or you were just running late—whether your taking us to your mom's for Thanksgiving dinner means you're picturing our future or you just needed a date to keep Mom quiet. Everything you do helps us to understand whether you're the sweet, caring, sensitive, trustworthy guy we're looking to spend the rest of our lives with—because those are the traits we want our husbands and our babies' daddies to possess.

Of course, it helps if he can make our toes curl. There isn't a woman on this earth who doesn't want her mate to turn her out on the regular. But you know what? If he's not the best lover in the world, but he's *all that* in every other aspect, we'd be willing to work with his boudoir skills.

That's not to say that some of us don't get strung out over the you-know-what. My girlfriend's sister Liz damn near lost her mind over this Negro who wasn't worth even a pinch of what he put her through. He'd disappear for weeks, then show up at the house with some tired present and an erection—the latter of which would get him back into her good graces every time. She's got two kids by him and a multitude of years of heartache and heartbreak. Still, she stays with him—one of the reasons being that he's good in bed.

Clearly, in Liz's case—or anyone else's like it—sexual chemistry doesn't mean jack if he's not going to take care of all the business. While there are a host of Lizzes out there, I'm certain that there are way more sistahs who are concerned with more than just a brother's sexual performance—the good traits that reveal for us whether we're making love with a man, or just strung out over some good sex. How about you all: **Will you guys stay in a relationship for good sex instead of looking for that special person with whom it will be transformed into making love?**

From a Brother

Depends on what you call "relationship." We'll keep coming around for good sex, that's for sure. Will we propose marriage? I highly doubt it.

We'll do plenty of things for the promise of good sex: drive cross-country on a skateboard, walk barefoot across a bed of crushed glass, sit through a three-hour concert of abstract free jazz, even pay good money to see a Broadway musical. If we don't think the woman is very interesting or pleasant to be around, we will reduce the time that we're with her and not having some of that good sex—but we will keep coming back. Until . . . we find the one. Then the whole equation changes. The good sex is long forgotten because now we're making love.

The difference between good sex and making love is like the difference between winning a pickup game and winning the NBA championship. It's like the difference between watching a Knicks game on television and sitting next to Spike at courtside. There just ain't no comparison.

To make love is something that every man wants to say he has done before he checks outta here. It is one of God's most glorious gifts to humankind. It is a feeling that has no parallel, transforming every fiber of your being into a quivering, orgasmic nerve ending.

When you have sex, your first thought after the fluid drains from you is where did you leave your keys and how long does protocol say you have to wait before you can start putting your clothes back on. Having sex is when you start thinking about your tax return and the performance of your mutual funds as Jimmy methodically slides in and out of a warm receptacle. When I was in college, my friends and I came up with the embarrassingly inelegant term "coyote fuck" to describe the kind of encounter that ended with you waking up with your left arm trapped beneath the sleeping head of a strange woman who, in the harsh light of morning or a powerful streetlamp, would put you in the mindset of a coyote who'd try to chew off his paw to get out of a trap.

And the only difference between sex and good sex is that with good sex you will lie down and cuddle—counting down the minutes until you can get up without inciting her ire—so she'll let you come back the next time you want some.

We like making love just as much as our female counterparts do. It is something we all strive for, even those of us currently running around clutching our thingies in our hands and shoving them anywhere they'll fit. It may take the thingie-clutchers a little longer to find it—or even recognize it when they find it—but they too want to make love.

You're My Guy, She's My Girl: Can't We All Just Get Along?

From a Sistah

Think oil and vinegar, water and fire—cats and dogs. Our sistah-girlfriends tend to get along with our men about as well as any of those combinations.

In fact, friends—whether they be ours or yours—are a sticky subject that causes grief in many a relationship. Frankly, we're a little leery of your boys, too—particularly the single ones who insist on dragging you all out for your little secret escapades about town, the ones who offer to "hook you up," tell you you don't need to be in a serious relationship, insist that you "play the field." Oh yeah, your little friends can get you in a heap a trouble with us sistahs.

And there is absolutely nothing harder for a sistah to pull off than the delicate balancing act that comes with trying to meld the friendship you have with your girlfriend with the relationship you have with your man. Girlfriend wants to stick to her role—shoulder to cry on, ear to twist, giggle partner—and boyfriend wants her to simply stick it. You all accuse her of being the bigmouth, the stool pigeon, the rabble-rouser—the one who jacks up your game. Meanwhile, we sistahs just sit back, bury our face in our hands and ask this simple question: **What do you have against our relationships with our girlfriends?**

From a Brother
We don't trust them—that's what's wrong with your girlfriends.

They tell you what you want to hear. If they don't have a man, they want you to be as miserable as they are. If they have any feelings at all toward me, they hate me for not picking them.

Ridiculous, you say? Well, how many times, after you've just called it quits with that boyfriend who thoroughly broke your heart, has your girlfriend chimed in to say she never did like him and is glad that you wised up and hit him in the ass with the door? I see you nodding your head as you count the many times. See, what this demonstrates is that all during the relationship, she was secretly sticking pins in the Ken and Barbie dolls she kept hidden under her bed, hoping she would have her best girlfriend returned to the same state of misery that she's in.

It's when the troubles move closer to home that a different set of emotions and instincts rises to the surface. You get selfish. You long for the days when you and your girl could run out to the mall, shop for three hours, giggle about the men you saw, then run back to your respective homes and talk on the phone for another three hours. When one of the two gets a man and the other doesn't . . . well, the phone calls get a little shorter. And one of the two is getting her bell rung a few times a week. Nothing worse than commiserating about your awful sex life with somebody whose thrice-weekly 1:00 A.M. screams of pleasure could set off car alarms.

And let's talk about logistics for a minute. There aren't many things that the three of us can do together that will make the three of us happy. We don't want to go shopping; girliefriend doesn't want to see *Terminator III* and watch us hold hands. We don't want to eat at the new gourmet soul food restaurant with the cute waiters; homegirl doesn't want to hit the sports bar and watch the playoff game over some brews. Where shall the twain meet?

If you don't carefully balance your activities between man and girl, somebody's going to be unhappy. If you decide to make the man unhappy, you endanger the relationship and cause him to wonder if your girl is more important than he is. If you choose your man over the girl, she's going to be pissed and secretly work to have the whole thing come crashing to an end. So either way, one of the most important people in your life is going to be unhappy with the choices you have made and make you pay for it.

Sometimes the girlfriend even makes moves on the man, either because she really likes him or maybe because she hates him and wants to kill the relationship. If this happens, it puts the man in the precarious position of trying to decide whether he should report the girlfriend to the proper authorities and risk the consequences—like his woman not believing him or accusing him of somehow leading her friend on—or keep quiet and run the risk that your woman might get wind of something and start becoming suspicious.

When I was in college, a girlfriend of my girlfriend kissed me flush on the lips once while we were dancing at a party and my woman had gone to the bathroom. I stared at her in horror, not understanding why she would do something like that and put us both in danger. If my girlfriend had seen the kiss, no doubt I would have been without a source of nightly warmth and the two of them would have been friends no more. I couldn't understand what would motivate a best friend to do something like that to her friend's man. I knew I wasn't THAT irresistible.

I think men, despite the lengthy catalogue of our problems and faults, would never think of initiating such a bold sexual advance with the woman of a best friend. We would be more likely to respect certain people and things as off-limits—I hope.

So why do women get so upset when their best friend finds a new man and wants to spend most of her time with him? After all, I thought y'all were supposed to be so romantic—and isn't that the height of romance?

From a Sistah

If there was one thing that we've learned in the age of Waiting to Exhale, *it's that sistah–girlfriend bonding is as important to most black women as their romantic relationships.*

They're our girls: We laugh together, cry together, get mad together, glad together, pray together—and we keep each other sane in a world full of people standing at the ready to make a sistah go raving mad.

So we take each other's advice very seriously—twirl it around as we deliberate on everything from what color shoes to wear with the green dress to, yes, which guy is right for us. We trust her because we know she has our best interests in mind—or at least we hope she does. She sees what's going on objectively—or at least we hope she does. And in some cases, she may have some insider 411 on the new guy in our life—or at least we hope she does. We need assurances: someone to hold our hands as we embark on unchartered territory, someone's smile to tell us we did well for ourselves, someone to play detective with us when we think he's messin' up, and someone's shoulder to cry on when he messes up—and we turn to the people we trust. More than often, it's our girls.

Of course, this can pose problems. No woman—whether she be a woman's best friend or her mama—should have that much dap in a woman's life that she has the power to make or break another woman's feelings for a man. Only the two people involved in a relationship can make that decision—and it should come without outside influences who may not know the real deal. But we do know of instances where we let our judgment lapse, lose our damn minds, and misguidedly let homegirl call the shots—prodding us into making bad relationship decisions. Some of them can be downright duplicitous; they'll bust up a sistah's relationship quick, fast and in a hurry, with the worst intentions—namely to take the place of her girl on that man's arm. Others, no matter what you may think, aren't as calculating; they're simply looking out for their girl's best interest.

I had a girlfriend, Denise, who thought she was doing her best to help our girlfriend Mona when she prodded her to break up with her man, Kent. See, Denise, Mona and Kent were out for dinner at a popular New York restaurant when some chick strolled up in there with her girlfriends, peeped Kent hugged up with Mona, then kindly walked up to Kent and smacked the mess out of him. It didn't take a rocket scientist to figure out that girlfriend was smacking Kent because she had just found out that the monogamous relationship she *thought* she had with him wasn't, well, monogamous. But Mona kindly sat down for dinner with Kent's cheating behind and acted as if nothing happened— much to Denise's chagrin. For the next few weeks after that, Denise called Mona every dumb so-and-so in the book, trying her best to convince her girlfriend to break up with that no-good-son-of-a-you-know-what Kent. Needless to say, Denise's constant insults and ridicule put a serious strain on her and Mona's relationship. And in the end, Kent got the boot, too—although he never did admit to the fact that the reason homegirl's hand connected with the side of his face was because he was busted cheating.

See, Denise's intentions were pure; she didn't want her girl's heart to continue to be stomped by a man who didn't respect her enough to tell her she wasn't the only one he was dating. Still, her constant sistah-girlfriend advice put a strain on all of their relationships—and I'm sure Kent wasn't digging her too much, either.

But you know what? The instances when this happens seem all too rare. We sistahs instead tend to look at our girlfriends as our ready ally—the one who will listen to our side of the story and nod in agreement with everything we say when you mess up. She listens when we need the undivided attention we couldn't get from you during that argument, ready to lend the much-needed, "That's right girl! You don't have to take that!" She's also the one who can put it painfully in perspective when we know we're wrong but refuse to admit it. She's that little angel on our shoulder, the one who distinguishes right from wrong for us. Above all else, though, she's simply our girl. The last thing we sistahs want to do is to have our best girlfriends—the ones who have been there for us through thick and thin—thinking that as soon as we get some, we lose our minds and forget all about the ones who have stuck by us through thick and thin. When we need a break from you, she's our welcome relief. And when we simply need her, she's there. So answer us this question: **How can we get you and our girlfriends to like each other?**

From a Brother
Make more of an effort to have us look at each other as friends rather than enemies.

Perhaps to get the ball rolling, you can pick a few events that we might both enjoy attending, such as a hit movie, a basketball game, a concert. You might have to brace yourself for one or two slightly tense or uncomfortable evenings in the beginning, but in the long run I believe it'll pay off, for several reasons:

1. Your girlfriend starts to see the man as a human being rather than a gruff voice on the phone, and she might start to see why you would be so attracted to him. This would make her less likely to try sabotage to get her shopping partner back. (Though, of course, it could backfire and she could fall in love with your man. I didn't say these were risk-free.)

2. Your man starts to see your girlfriend as a human being rather than an annoying little pest who calls at the most inopportune times and keeps you on the phone even past the hour of BET's nasty love videos. This would make him less likely to try to pressure you into losing her phone number, and you'll no longer have to sneak behind his back to call or see her. (This too could backfire, especially if your girlfriend comes equipped with a big butt and a smile. So if that's the case, keep an eye out for the release of some poison.)

3. What could be better than you and your buddy and your beau having a great time together? It'll make your life so much easier. If he has enough fun, you might even convince him to go along with you guys to the mall every once in . . . okay, I take that back. He'll never go to the mall with the two of you. But he'll be more tolerant of your shopping trips—if, of course, you don't cause the credit card to burst into flames from overuse.

4. When you and your man inevitably hit a few bumps in the road, your girlfriend will be at roadside trying to repair any damage instead of tossing out more boulders for you to slam into. Having her on the side of your relationship is a rare and remarkable thing. Not only does she let you lean on her shoulder, she can even offer advice that springs from her knowledge of the man in question. Usually in these situations, the girlfriend's advice comes from the memory of how Larry dogged her last year. In all circumstances, the worst thing in the world for your continuing love is for your girl to start thinking about Larry.

5. If she was with y'all all evening, she won't call you with a desperate need to talk for two hours just as you're about to get your swerve on.

Intimidation: Why Does He Keep Running Away?

From a Sistah

Sistah + education + business suit + high income = no man.

At least that's what all too many successful, middle-class, hardworking black women are complaining about more and more these days. The general perception among independent, white-collar sistahs is that brothers who have the same as they—the material and social wealth that comes with the decent- and high-paying jobs—are increasingly falling into the slim-pickings category.

One need only walk down a block during evening rush hour in a major city to see their point: Clusters of black men stand idle, with nothing filling their hands but the inside of their pockets and a whole lot of time. And the sistahs from that same neighborhood climb off the bus or out of the subway, arms full with briefcases and groceries, feet clad in stocking-protector socks and sneakers, weary from a hard day's work, and walk past them on their way home—all too likely to settle onto the sofa, tired and alone.

And that gulf between the two is all too deep—ever-widening.

Take a look at the nation's college campuses, and that's borne out with every incoming freshman class, and every graduating one, too. It's anything but amusing to us sistahs, but the running joke among too many college-bound brothers is the ridiculous ratio of black women to black men at our intellectual institutions.

"Man, a brother could have his pick," they inflect, a gleam in their eyes.

This is not to say that every black man who isn't working in a white-collar job is an unemployed "corner keeper," or that every brother on a college campus is enrolled in Mo' Booty 101. It's to say that the more sistahs become successful in their careers, the fewer brothers there are keeping lockstep with them.

The sistahs who went to college and got good grades and graduated and worked hard to get those great jobs were raised to expect that there would be a brother with the same credentials waiting for them when they "made it."

All too often, the appearance is that it's not happening.

In some cases, the sistahs turn to what's available—go for the guy who doesn't have the best job, but is a hard worker nonetheless; doesn't have the titles, but walks tall; doesn't have the education, but has common sense.

And, for a while, she is happy—pleased as punch simply to have a man.

And, for a while, it is honorable—because she has let go of her white-house-and-a-picket fence notions, and plain gotten real.

And, for a while, it works.

And then, out of the blue, he is gone—turned off, suddenly, by the things she alternately worked so hard to get for herself and worked so hard to ignore when she realized he didn't have any of it for himself. She talks about taking a vacation to Paris, he broods that she's flaunting her money in his face. She takes him to the office party, he acts like the co-workers are looking down on him.

It is the I-N-T-I-M-I-D-A-T-I-O-N factor—and it's killing what little hope we independent, self-sufficient sistahs have for getting what we all want out of life—a good husband, some kids, a nice, happy life.

But perhaps our perception is wrong. **Are brothers intimidated by successful black women?**

From a Brother

Is there any record in the album of black male–female relations that gets as overplayed as this one, the intimidation thing? Are we intimidated? The first answer that comes to mind is "Hell no." But I understand that the situation is a lot more complicated than that.

This is another classic case of the two genders looking at the same incident and coming up with entirely different descriptions of what just happened. Sistahs are too quick to reach for the intimidation explanation when things go wrong. Brothers face some pretty scary stuff out there during the course of our days to be frightened by a sistah with a good job. Or even one with a "career." I suspect that there are other things, beneath-the-surface type things, that derail relationships when there appears to be a mismatch between the woman's accomplishments and the man's.

Conflicts over money are a big relationship derailer. This looms even larger when the woman makes more money. If money sinks a relationship, does that woman walk away saying the brother was "intimidated"? Control is another one. Is the woman trying to remake the brother into her buppie counterpart? That may be admirable, but what if that's not the kind of lifestyle to which he's aspiring? What if he's more comfortable at a bowling alley than jazz concert? If she refuses to go bowling and he doesn't want to accompany her to the Blue Note, the relationship will quickly find itself on the rocks. Was intimidation the culprit here, too? How about his friends and her friends? She thinks his are crude and uncouth; he believes hers are stuck-up and pretentious. Maybe they're both right and they can't find common ground on the issue. Is that about intimidation, too? In other words, different goals often represent a difference in priorities.

I'm a firm believer in the philosophy that we are intimidated by people who want us to be intimidated. I have certainly met enough accomplished women to see that while some are so intent on looking strong and in command that they come off as cold and unapproachable, others can be as warm and inviting as the morning sun. So I know they're out there—hardworking career women who realize there's no crime in being pleasant, that the feminist police won't hunt them down and revoke their membership card, that the failures of one or two (or even three) brothers shouldn't taint everyone who comes after them.

I'm sure there are brothers who feel a little uneasy around a woman who is more accomplished. It's only natural to feel a little insecure when confronted with any person, man or woman, who has done much better for himself or herself. But the key question is how you deal with those feelings of insecurity. Many successful women contend that the man quickly accuses them of trying to act like they're better than he is. They say that this male insecurity pops up in predictable and also unexpected ways, whether it's domestic violence or sullenness or cheating. And I'm sure all these things have occurred in situations where men were intimidated. These brothers need to check themselves before they try to deal with another high-powered career woman, perhaps set their sights a little lower. These men usually know up front whether they can hang or not. They should be able to sense that they aren't going to be able to get past her salary and job and education, and they should stay away, look for someone closer to their level. And if they have this crazy macho need to feel superior to their lady, they should go on down to the night school GED program and see what they can find when classes let out for the evening.

As for the rest of us, we are starting to think the intimidation claim is camouflage for other problems in the relationship. **If a blue-collar brother wants to stay blue-collar—bowling and beer instead of jazz clubs and white wine—and the career sistah isn't with that, does that mean the relationship is doomed because he's intimidated?**

From a Sistah

*The relationship **is** doomed if he can't put the bowling ball and beer bottle down every once in awhile and feel comfortable in a professional woman's wine-and-jazz-club world. Ditto if she can't let her hair down and keep score on league nights.*

Though I fully encourage professional sistahs to date blue-collar workers, I don't think such couplings are easy. There are simply instances where brothers won't be able to hang with the fact that they don't roll in the same circles as the sistah, and there may be sistahs who can't see themselves becoming comfortable in a world that's not as highbrow as they would like. It's just a fact of life—and no amount of forcing is going to get that square peg to fit comfortably into that circle.

This was a hot topic of debate during a relationships panel on which I participated with *Do Right Man* author Omar Tyree when *The Sistahs' Rules* first hit the bookstores. One sistah, nicely dressed, well-coiffed, stood up and lamented about how she tried her best to date a blue-collar brother, but he spent all of his time being bothered by her experiences. She said she'd excitedly told him about her trip to Paris, and he got an attitude. She'd excitedly asked him to help her hang a piece of art she bought, and he gave her fever.

She chalked it up to his being insecure—and rightfully so, I thought.

But Omar, himself from a blue-collar background, suggested something that I thought brilliant: He said that perhaps the brother was turned off by her constantly talking about things he couldn't relate to.

Maybe he'd never been to Paris," Omar said simply.

Indeed.

And if most of what she's talking about doesn't necessarily jibe with what he's familiar with, and he's not willing to open his mind and at least attempt to relate to what she's talking about, it's not going to work.

Now, Omar suggested that she hold back a little bit on the info—ease the brother into the finer things in life. I don't necessarily agree with that. No person, whether they're a professional woman or a blue-collar man, should be forced to hold back on discussing their experiences with their love interest out of fear that that person can't hang.

Perhaps you can make us sistahs understand what Omar was talking about that night in Brooklyn: **Why should we go out of our way to be nice to a blue-collar brother just to make him feel comfortable and better about himself?**

From a Brother

Why not? It's not about being patronizing or treating him like a vulnerable child. It's about being pleasant and tender so he feels good not only about himself but also about you and your relationship.

That question would be like us asking, "Why do I have to wrap my arms around her and tell her I love her just because she had a horrible day and is on the verge of tears when she comes home?" No one would tell us we HAD to give her a hug, but if we consistently fought the notion that we should give her love in her times of need, we'd be spending the rest of our days nurturing a growing relationship with Mr. Budweiser and *Penthouse* magazine. These are the things that lovers do for each other. They provide each other support. They provide warmth. They are NICE.

Do these sistahs really think they're going to have much luck finding a rich, successful man who doesn't mind putting up with their hostility and neck-rolling attitude? These brothers will be even more picky than the garbage man who decides he's going to give the corporate lawyer sistah a try. So, at the very least, these sistahs might consider their relationship with the blue-collar brother as practice for when they actually do snag their Brother Mr. Right in the shiny white Benz. Because if they don't practice being nice, warm and friendly, they'll unhappily discover that when they need these character traits, they'll dip into the well and come back with a bucket full of arsenic.

Remember what our mamas said: If you keep your face frowned up like that, it might just stay that way.

Finding Time for Each Other

From a Sistah

Quality time and all your time are synonymous to us. What else do you all have to do besides spend your every waking moment thinking about being with us—breathing us?

We don't want you all up in our faces all day, every day. Just most of the free day.

What, you got something else to do? Somebody else to be with? You tired of me or something? These, dear, are all the questions we ask ourselves when you find something else to do besides what we want you to do with us. See, the way we figure it, you should be happy going to the movies, or planting in the garden, or washing the car, or going shopping or going to church or going out to dinner or going over to Angelou's or watching paint dry—so long as it's with us.

And why not?

You're my man, right? I love you, right? You love me, right? We're in this together, right? So we're figuring you want to spend your spare time with us—at least some of it.

But Lord knows it doesn't work out that way. A brother could work five long days of the week—put in a ton of overtime and walk into his apartment dog-tired every night at 11:00 P.M., spend Friday night out drinking beer with the boys, spend Saturday morning playing tennis with his boys, spend Saturday afternoon washing his car over at his boy's house, take a break from his boys by taking his honey-pie out to the movies or to dinner or wherever, then spend all day Sunday in front of the television watching the game, scratching himself, burping, drinking beer and arguing with the refs, with—who else?—his boys.

Then he wonders why his girlfriend is all salty and stuff when he says he spends more than enough time with her.

News flash—three hours on Saturday evening does not constitute quality time. It constitutes fitting-you-in time—and we sistahs are quite confused, boyfriend, with brothers' accusations that we monopolize their time.

Perhaps I'm underplaying the amount of time we actually spend with you brothers—perhaps I'm exaggerating how much time you spend with your boys. Just a little. I mean, you all are pretty interested in spending all your time with us when you first get into a relationship with us. Take, for instance, when Nick and I first started dating. We both lived in Brooklyn, but our apartments were in different neighborhoods. That didn't stop us from getting together almost every night and every weekend, though. Whoever got home from work first would usually call the other's answering machine to make plans for the evening—whether it entailed cooking dinner, renting a video or strolling along the Brooklyn Heights Promenade. We just couldn't get enough of each other. We **had** to be together.

It's the feeling, I always thought, that lovers shared—the constant need for one to be around the other.

Our craving for one another eventually led to us moving in together. We figured, why waste all that money paying two rents —particularly when we only used one apartment during the course of most evenings? It just made fiscal sense—let alone love sense.

But Nick was an anomoly. Other brothers? Huh—you'd think the time they put in with their girlfriends was all the time they had in the world. And let her work her mouth to ask him if she could have a little bit more time: Boyfriend might as well walk around with shackles on his ankles, because he will proclaim himself a slave to his woman—a man barren of time outside of his relationship.

We don't get it—this whole concept brothers have about us sistahs monopolizing their time. Brothers are always screaming about how we should be happy with the quality time they spend with us, and that we should stop tripping over the fact that he's refusing to spend *all* his time with us. Just what the hell is quality time anyway? Isn't the time you spend with your girlfriend— whether it be two minutes, two hours or two days with her— quality time? **What's the difference in a brother's mind between a lot of time and quality time—and which one matters more?**

From a Brother

The problem with the distinction between more time and quality time is that the man and the woman might disagree from day to day, hour to hour, minute to minute, on the definition of quality time. Brotherman might think those two hours watching the game together were the most meaningful hours they spent all week; sistah might have thought the same thing about the two hours they spent snuggled on the couch reading separate magazines. All that being said, I think quality time is more important than a lot of time because quality time is going to be more memorable and have more of an impact on the relationship.

The devil is in the details. The key to this question is whether we agree on our definitions. That takes more than just good communication—how often are we going to turn to our mate after spending time with her and say, "I think I would label today's activities as quality time"?—it also requires that you know your mate well enough to be able to accurately predict the way she'd define the time spent together in various situations.

Quality time requires the partners to have planned the time together in advance. Quality time means we are fully aware of the other person's presence at all times; we are enjoying the other person's space no matter where we are and what we are doing.

During the writing of this book, my wife and I spent a great deal of time together in the same apartment, but we were usually in separate rooms working on separate computers. I do not consider this quality time—which is probably why we enjoyed it so much when we could turn off the computers and actually come together to bask in each other's presence, whether it was in front of the television or just talking in the bedroom. The purpose of the togetherness was to be together, not to accomplish some other task or view some event.

I think men sometimes fall into the trap of confusing the two and not understanding why our mates are unhappy with us. It's easy to get this way—we grow tired on the job and we sometimes don't want to think about making an effort to enjoy our spouse's company. Isn't it just good enough that we're together in the same house? Why do I have to make a conscious effort to entertain you or take special note of your company? Can't I just sit here next to you in front of the television and keep the company of my beer?

But when we're together but silent and untouching, we might as well be apart. We gain no physical sustenance from the other person, no soulful uplift from conversation, no pleasure from the other person's smile or smell, nothing. We both become lumps of clay, unmoving and unmoved, taking up space in each other's realm without making even the tiniest impact on that space—unless we happen to emit unpleasant odors or sounds.

But sometimes when we're together and silent and untouching, we're still acutely aware of and enjoying the hell out of the other person. This can get confusing.

Because men seem to have a higher threshold for the continued presence of lumps of clay, we might take much longer than our sistahs to realize that the relationship has been sucked dry of quality time. That even if the amount of time together is significant, it still doesn't amount to much more than time. Hours on end, dry, stifling, uninspiring, tortorous—and there we are, grinning away in our blissful ignorance.

There's not much point to marriage or emotional attachment if we're not going to uplift and occasionally resurrect each other's souls. We might as well go through this thing by ourselves without that. As an aunt of mine used to say, "I can do bad by myself."

How do we know when it qualifies as quality time in the sistah book?

From a Sistah

Just the other day, Nick and I decided to go to the movies before we sat down and tied ourselves to the computers—again. And then, somewhere between our rolling out of bed and our hitting the showers, we decided we should go into Morristown, a quaint suburban enclave in Morris County, N.J., to shop for a new car. And then we started figuring, might as well see if we can check out a restaurant for lunch while we're there—because we rarely eat anywhere in New Jersey besides the towns around South Orange and Newark.

It was beautiful outside—the first cloudless spring day on which the sun was shining and the air was warm and you could smell the blossoms in the air. I decided I was going to wear white, in honor of the day. Then I found myself putting on a little lipstick and a little eye shadow and a little mascara (Nick will readily attest to the fact that I never do this on a weekend because I can't be so bothered on my days off)—and I realized I was excited because I was going to ride in the truck, with the music blasting and the windows rolled down, the air whistling through my braids, with my man.

What's the big deal, you ask? Let me tell you: We never ride in that thing unless we are rushing to the train station or rushing to a reading or rushing to a friend's house for dinner or rushing to some event that we promised to attend. Hardly ever do we ride in the truck in unknown territory, on a beautiful spring day, with no destination in particular.

I was so content that day. And the funny thing about it is we didn't do anything special—it wasn't a big production. We were just happy—a couple in love just chillin'. We found ourselves giggling and holding hands and marveling at how awesome it was to just spend an entire quiet day together, because it's so incredibly rare.

And we sistahs wish that every day could be like this.

Alas, we know that it can't. With the technology age slapping us in the face and the increasing demands of our jobs on our time, it's damn near impossible. We spend an amazing amount of our days and weeks being team players—going in early to work, leaving late, working weekends to get the job done and make the boss happy—and by the time we get home, our energy is spent entirely too much to be bothered with spending some quality time with our mates.

But we sistahs feel that we have to make that quality time anyway—"that quality time" meaning you are spending it with us, paying attention to us, letting us know that right now, at this minute, you don't want to be anywhere else but with your girl.

That feeling can come during a fifteen-minute walk around the block after dinner, or on a lazy Sunday afternoon, when we sit in the bed with *The New York Times* spread across the sheets and read each other something interesting we just stumbled across in an article. It can come during a two-hour tour of a museum, where we critically discuss each piece of art, or it can come during the half hour we hold hands while we watch that horror flick at the Saturday matinee.

It doesn't seem that much to ask for—though sometimes brothers act as if those simple pleasures are tantamount to a round in the dentist's chair. **Do brothers ever see the lack of quality time as a problem in the relationship—or do they see it as a blessing?**

From a Brother

It's certainly not a blessing if it's going to result in our woman trying to restrict our movements, our free time, our leisure activities, because she thinks we've been spending too much time away from home. We know we have to maximize quality time as much as possible if we're going to be able to keep any of our time away from work as our own.

The way it happens is this: we've been working overtime nearly every night over the course of two weeks. Our wife is complaining that she misses us, that we're not able to have any fun together anymore or do anything interesting. Our regular golf or tennis or basketball or bowling or hunting or fishing or sailing buddy is also yapping in the other ear that the weather is just great and he's sorry that we're not getting a chance to participate in one of our life's most pleasurable activities. We know we're going to have a totally free Saturday coming up. Dilemma: Who gets the time, the wife or the recreational activity? If we choose the activity, the wife is going to be pissed and she'll make it that much harder the next time we want to go out and play. If we choose the wife, the buddy will get over it in a matter of minutes—but we probably won't, especially if we don't see another free Saturday on the horizon anytime soon. In this situation, most of us do the wise thing and pick the wife because we won't be able to bear the freeze in our house that will result if we don't. We don't particularly like wearing gloves in the summer, but that's how cold our house will get if we go out and play golf if she's been planning a day at the beach.

With this in mind, we have to make every possible situation into quality time, so that we'll have a positive balance in the bank. Get enough of those suckers saved up and we'll be able to play tennis from sunup to sundown when that free Saturday comes. And we must be sure to communicate to her as subtly as possible that we are making these sacrifices for her because we really just want to make her happy. After that, she'll understand that the tennis day is due us after we went to the mall with her on Thursday night after working three hours OT, then came home late on Friday night and dragged ourselves into the kitchen to make her dinner. Just the week before, we accompanied her to the Meryl Streep film festival rather than racing to the new Bruce Willis movie on opening night and watching him blow stuff up. We've got so much quality time in the bank that she wanted to check our temperature when we offered to cook.

My wife and I have been having some of these struggles over my tennis habit. If I could, I'd play tennis every night during the week and every morning on weekends. But in a marriage, such a schedule just isn't very practical or possible. For the most part, my spouse is understanding of my tennis jones and she tends to be pretty tolerant—that is, until I went a little too far on Easter. I thought I was doing all right by putting on my Easter finery and attending church with my wife, my sister Angelou and my brother-in-law James. In the back of my head, even during the Easter sermon, I must admit, I was wondering what time I'd be able to get out there on the tennis court. Imagine my chagrin when I found out the crew was planning to go out and partake in a grand Easter dinner. I explained that I couldn't go, trying not to see the deep frown on my honey's face. I was almost on the verge of changing my mind, but then I thought about how much I needed to practice my backhand slice down the line—that shot can come in very handy on the service return—and so I went forward with my plans, saying goodbye to the three of them as they went off to enjoy a dinner while I headed to the courts. Besides the fact that it was Easter Sunday, another error I had made was playing tennis for at least the three or four consecutive days before Easter. Not even catching on at that point, I played again on Monday night. Needless to say, I was in such a disastrous state of arrears in my quality time bank account that I was still in the red months later, hesitantly seeking permission for just a simple ninety-minute after-work hit-around. I'm convinced that because of our screwup on Easter Sunday and the several days before and after Easter, my regular partner and friend James O'Neal and I developed a reputation among our spouses and friends as tennisaholics who don't have enough sense to know when to put down the racquet for a minute. We'd probably have been out there even more over the past months if not for the Easter faux pas. None of this meant that we loved our wives any less. We just love tennis. And we should have been more aware of the balance in our quality time bank accounts. When it's getting precariously close to zero or if there are numbers with a negative sign in front, it's time to make some deposits—otherwise, that woman we love and whose anger we desperately want to avoid will start finding regular reasons to rage.

Skeletons

From a Sistah

Eddie Murphy talked about them—remember? Had this hilarious standup routine where he gigged about skeletons in the closet, and how every once in a while, a big ole juicy bone'll just fall right on out of our mouths in midsentence—just drop on the floor like a ten-pound boulder.

Skeletons, of course, are the little secrets from our past—the crap that only you, the person you did it with and God (hopefully) know about. And most of us have the common sense to keep it that way—particularly when it comes to our new mates. We pretty much know that when we're vacationing with the new one in the Bahamas, we don't need to go into details about how we got sand in places other than between our toes when we last traveled to the island with our ex-beaus. It's pretty much a given that when you pass by the dark building on State Street—the one with the pillars that were big and dark enough to hide your public sexual escapade with Jerome—you don't need to relive the experience with Tyrone.

Obvious.

But it's those little bones—the chicken wings/wishbones—that jack us up every time. We think we're sharing a private joke, an intimate moment with the guy we're looking to get with, and all of a sudden, "Houston? We have a problem." Like, to this day, my husband won't get off of something I barely remember telling him about my college experience. It came up in a simple conversation about weight, something about how I haven't seen the other side of 100 pounds since college.

"I was ninety-eight pounds," I reminisced, "and even then, I thought I was fat. But then again, all of my friends on the football team thought it was great fun to bench-press me—so I guess, in retrospect, I wasn't all that big."

Well, what did I give him that little piece of information for? Money's still giving me grief over it.

I didn't think that was a big deal. It was cute, I thought it was funny and I had no earthly clue that it was going to set some stuff off in the Millner-Chiles household. Who knew? I mean, I could think of a million other things that I did in college and beyond that would probably set his little world on fire—none of which, obviously, I will go into here, because it's all official black history, right?—but this, no, it wasn't supposed to start no junk.

Which, of course, makes it very difficult for us to figure out whether we should just hide everything from you all and pretend like we had no human contact with the male species until we met beautiful you.

So I guess what we need to know from you is this: Is there anything in our past love life that's safe to talk about?

From a Brother

Well, we may be able to tolerate a story or two about the little boy you liked in fifth grade, or even the one with the jheri curl in ninth grade—as long as you never removed the panties during "doctor" and neither one of them got any substantial play. It's not that we won't want to hear about all this stuff—in fact, some of us may crave the information—it's just that it messes with our head so much once we do.

Details about your past escapades provide us with the ability to imagine you with somebody else, "doin' it." It's a nightmare image for us (except perhaps for those kinky dudes who like to watch their women with someone else. They deserve their own chapter—in somebody else's book). It's almost as bad as actually stumbling upon you humping somebody else in our bed. Okay, maybe it's not that bad.

But anyway, this all may sound silly and illogical to you because you know we realize that you're hardly coming to us as virgins. But if we have too much information our imagination manages to torture us on a regular basis. That's why it's especially worse if we've met the guy or he happens to be a friend of ours. There's no way we can escape that one—Raheem thrusting away on top of our girl. I'm getting mad just writing about it—and I don't even have a friend named Raheem.

Boys don't like to share. You've probably noticed this after a five-minute visit to the local playground. Some boys eventually have their stinginess beaten out of them by parents, siblings, or so-called "friends," but even they probably pledge that once they become grownups they're never going to share anything with any-body—lawnmowers, dirty videotapes, baseball mitts. We might do it once in a while, but we hand it over begrudgingly with detailed instructions about when we'd like to have it back. So imagine how we feel about sharing our women. That'd be even worse than letting somebody drive our car.

When our mates let slip a little skeleton, even if it's as small as a chicken wing or wishbone, it reminds us that we are getting used goods. That may be an inelegant way of putting it, but what it means is that someone else has gotten there first. They beat us to it. Maybe even quite a few somebody elses. The more somebody elses we find out about, the less happy we will be.

When my lovely wife let slip the line about being bench-pressed by the football team, a flood of images rushed back to me about the kind of women at the college I attended who would let the football players bench-press them. I didn't have a very high opinion of these women; I thought if they allowed themselves to be bench-pressed they would allow the football team to do a lot of other, more intimate things. I never imagined that I was married or engaged to one of these women. I have been informed by my lovely wife that my stereotypes about these kind of women are completely inaccurate and stupid, and that in no way did she do anything with the football team I might have imagined in my sick little mind. Okay. I'll accept that. Maybe I was reading too much into her little skeleton. But I couldn't help but wonder when we attended the wedding of one of her classmates a bit later and there were quite a few extra-large men in attendance—they could only fit about three to a pew—if any of them had bench-pressed my wife.

Speaking of my wife, I AM quite curious to know much more about the "million other things" she did in college that would set my little (why does my world have to be "little?") world on fire. Something tells me I'll never get much more than a couple of the million, and she'll have to be staring at the bottom of a tequila bottle to let the skeletons drop. That's probably just as well. I couldn't take another 999,999 bench-press stories, anyway.

I don't think there's anything a woman can do to change us on this—unless you happen to be married to one of those kinky dudes who gets off on hearing every gory detail. I don't happen to be one of those dudes. Neither are any of the brothers I know—unless they're hiding it from me. The safest bet for sistahs would be to squelch all talk of past sexual dalliances. If your man is pressing you real hard, make up a wild, fantastical story about being pleasured by an entire frat party. Then tell him you were just kidding. He'll be 99 percent sure that you ARE just kidding—but that tiny 1 percent that's not sure will make him feel so miserable that he'll recognize he doesn't need to press you on any more details unless he wants to be tortured by these unwanted images for the rest of his life. And then one day you'll both be at a cocktail party and he'll see you rush up and hug some guy you're obviously pleased as punch to see. He'll walk up and stick out his hand, and you'll introduce the fellow as an old college buddy—who was the frat brother of an old boyfriend. The made-up frat story will come rushing back to him and he'll have to run outside for air. You won't even remember the frat story, of course. But it will have served its purpose, again and again.

Don't you sistahs get upset when you hear a detailed story about one of our old loves—or if you meet her?

From a Sistah

So long as you're not all smiling and grinning while you're reminiscing, everything is smooth daddy with us.

We like to hear all the old dirt about who you slept with and what you all did and what you liked about her—and particularly what you didn't like about her. And if we get the 4-1-1 and then just happen to get put into a situation where we're in the same room with her?

Yeah, buddy.

See, we're completely not like you guys in that respect; we don't get bothered by the idea that you've been with someone before us. We know your reputations as men, and it would be downright ignorant for us to assume that you'd had absolutely no or very little carnal knowledge before you got to us.

It is no surprise, therefore, that you have memories of ex-girlfriends and ex-lovers—the little chippies who turned you on and turned you out, took you, as Stevie said, "riding in the rocket," then dropped your "black ass back down to this cold, cold world."

And we want to—actually need to—hear all about it. The reasons are simple:

1. We can be sure not to repeat her mistakes, and figure out what you want from us in the process. If you dropped her because she was a nag, or she ran up your credit card bills or she didn't put enough cream in your coffee—if you know what I mean—then we know to let you work at your own reasonable pace, to charge only a respectable amount on your American Express card and to make sure your coffee is creamed on the regular—if you know what I mean. It's a learning tool for us. And seeing as you brothers don't usually offer up enough info on that front, we can pick up from the clues you drop in your relationship-gone-sour stories. This, of course, can work against you, too, as we can find out a few of your faults in those stories—and use them to book up in the same direction sistah-girl did when she realized she couldn't deal with your mess, either.

2. We've got the inside scoop on her when she comes in our direction. May be a bit catty, but hey—I'm just trying to keep it real. If sistah-girl walks into the room in that fly Tahari suit—the one we saw in Bloomingdale's with that $425 price tag—but we know girlfriend couldn't afford bubbles for her bathwater, it makes us feel a little bit better as we hang onto your arm looking sharp as a tack. If she's flirting obsessively with every man in the room, we know it's because she's uncomfortable seeing us on your arm. And we hope she done gained a good fifty pounds, her weave ain't as tight as it was in them pictures we found in your old shoebox, and she's still clutching that broken-down Fendi bag you bought her back in 1978, not knowing you picked it up at the flea market. No, not all of us are this foul—but some of us enjoy this immensely.

3. Details are ammunition. That's right. Ammunition. It means that whatever you say will be held against you in the sistah court of law. You may be making an absolutely valid point that could win you that battle, but we can take it there with the dirt from your past relationships to win the war. A smart sistah knows to store the information away for a later date, then drop it like the A-bomb at the most opportune time. When you're telling me that I need to start contributing to the belt-tightening around our monthly budget by cutting back on the shoe-shopping sprees? I can rest assured that I'll shut you up by reminding you that I remember the time you spent your last dime trying to please her, and how she didn't appreciate a damn thing. "See how you do me? Shaniqua didn't give two dog bones about that Fendi bag you bought her, but I care about those Via Spiga pumps with the green suede trim, baby. I really do."

So come on, baby, tell me more. Don't hold back. Please.

And as for our skeletons, if we let one just sort of slip, does it automatically mean we're going to hear about it for the rest of our lives?

From a Brother

Nah, after a while we will probably stop reminding you about the fact that you told us—but we'll never forget.

A brother never forgets that indelible image of his woman with another man. It's seared there in his long-term memory to torture him whenever something triggers it (now you know why I start moaning and writhing on the couch everytime I watch a college football game, baby?).

In fact, this is one of the few things we actually do remember that could possibly be stored under the category of ammunition. We will talk about arguing a little later, but one of the reasons we often decide not to argue points is that we forget every one of your transgressions or faux pas that could be used against you. (So when you're tossing out a list of our failures and we're trying to recall whether we actually did leave the toilet seat up seven days in a row three months ago—or if you're just making it up—we're trying to think of something equally uncaring you've done to us and coming up with blanks. We wave you off with a snort and you think that we either have given up—which is true—or that we just don't want to argue with you—which is also true. But if we could just remember a few of your damn screwups, we'd be much more likely to at least take the argument into a second round rather than throw in the towel after you land the first shot to the head.)

But skeletons we remember. Whether we throw them in your face from time to time will depend on you—if you give us a reason to need some ammunition. As for the pain that the skeletons initially cause us, that will fade over time. So you don't need to fear that your skeleton is going to cause permanent psychic damage.

Actually, we might even be tempted to let the skeleton go if we meet the dude one day and he turns out to look nothing like the way you described him. Instead of a cross between Maxwell and Chico Debarge, homeboy looks more like a cross between Chico and The Man. If that's the case, we feel satisfied that there's no way in hell he smoothed you out better than we do, not with that Godzilla breath and body by Chips Ahoy. Of course, if he really does look like a cross between Maxwell and Chico, then you might find yourself wondering the next day why we're hyperventilating on the floor from trying to complete a situp.

But none of this is intended to keep you from sharing the pivotal moments of your past life with us. Don't worry about hurting our feelings; tell us all the freaky stories. We can take it. We might even be impressed to know our partner could find such a creative use for a jar of peanut butter.

Cohabitation: How Do You Feel About Shacking Up?

From a Sistah

We had had a longtime relationship. We had planned, basically, to be together. We met in college, and dated for quite a while after. Only one thing was keeping us from doing this forever-relationship thing: distance. I lived in Albany, N.Y., a good four-hour drive away from where he lived in Long Island, N.Y., where I grew up. I had moved to Albany after college to work for the Associated Press. It was a job with tremendous opportunities for me as a young journalist. It was hard maintaining a relationship with him while I was all the way up there—hard maintaining any relationships, for that matter, as all of my family and friends lived downstate, in the New York City and Long Island areas—but we managed to work it out.

Then I got the call: An editor at the *Daily News* wanted to interview me for a position as a City Hall reporter. I was excited because it was the big time—a chance to work at one of the largest newspapers in the country, in one of the most prestigious positions a reporter could ever have, particularly a twenty-four-year-old reporter. But I was apprehensive, because I'd worked for the AP for three years and I was perfectly happy with my job and my life—and frankly, I was afraid that I wasn't quite ready for the big-time.

After turning it around in my mind, pondering it with my parents and praying about it, I asked my then boyfriend what he thought about the move. Of course, he was excited, because for him it would mean that the distance that separated us would automatically be whittled into a short half-hour trip, rather than the four hours it took for us to get to one another. For me, though, it would have meant much more than that: If I moved, we were going to do this.

"So," I said hesitantly, "if I take this job, I'm thinking maybe we could live together. I mean, we're going to be together, finally, and it's time to move to a higher level anyway. Right?"

"Move in together?" he said. "You and me?"

I'm thinking to myself, "No, me and yo' mama," but talking about his mama wasn't going to help the situation, so I said, "Yes. You and me. Living together. How about it?"

"I don't think so," he said.

I was taken aback. What was this "I don't think so" crap? Had we not dated (on and off) for a good five years? Had we not talked about our future together, our plans, our hopes and dreams? Was this Negro out of his natural-born mind?

"Why not?" I said.

"Because if I get tired of you, I won't have anywhere to go."

And that was that. Homeboy was as serious as a heart attack; this man had no desire whatsoever for us to lay what I considered to be the groundwork for our future together.

See, shacking up was everything to me. Yes, it would have been tantamount to living in sin (for some people), like allowing him to forgo buying the cow because the milk was free. I've heard it all—but I stood by and continue to stand by my philosophy: The only way to truly get to know a man is to live with him. You can smell his dragon breath in the morning, peep out his penchant for dropping his dirty drawers in the middle of the floor in the afternoon, and catch on to his attitude shifts in the evenings— none of which you truly catch while you're dating and living separately because everybody, you see, is on good behavior. He brushes his teeth every time before he sees you, but does he brush his teeth every morning? There are no dirty dishes in his sink when you come over twice a week, but damn if they don't turn to stone from sitting in the sink for weeks on end when you're not around. You may see zero evidence of other women while you're visiting— but are Shaniqua, Shalinda and Sharonda going to stop calling him when your name is on the lease? Oh, you may not recognize his monster butt—and it will be up to you to decide if you want to deal with monster butt for the rest of your life, or if you want him to go by way of Godzilla—back to sea.

For good.

So I took it personal when he said he didn't want to live with me—just knew he had something to hide—a problem with me— that he didn't want to do this relationship thing, or that he, at the very least, wasn't serious about it. I thought that it said a mountain of things about how he felt about me and our future together.

Was I right? **Do brothers think it's cool to live with a person they're serious about?**

From a Brother

I'm not going to front—deciding to live with a woman is scary as hell. But it's probably just a little less scary than actually walking down the aisle, which means it's a fairly effective way for us to ease out of bachelorhood—like taking methadone to break a heroin addiction.

Or like a practice run before the marathon. It gives you a solid idea of whether you are ready for the long haul, the big kahuna. And it also tells you whether this is the right woman or if you were just fooling yourself all along. Lastly, it forces you to confront the reality of monogamy and whether you're ready for it before you've signed the marriage certificate and it's too late to change your mind.

I've been involved in three cohabitation situations, and two of them eventually led to marriage. In each one I picked up valuable information about myself and the other woman that proved quite useful for me in deciding whether this was someone with whom I could spend the rest of my life. Only once, with the first marriage, did I turn out to be wrong.

Most men have never shared close living quarters with a woman who sees herself as our equal. Mom certainly didn't. In childhood, older and younger sisters didn't—they either thought they could dominate us or we could dominate them. So here comes this woman who appears to be perfect in every way suddenly telling us we need to clean the bathroom or come straight home after work instead of going out for beers. If we're going to be a few hours late, we have to remember to pull out the cell phone and check in with our new dispatcher. That new number blowing up our pager is our own.

Some of us don't respond well to these changes. Some of us want to live carefree and irresponsibly a little longer, sharing our bathrooms with spiders and cobwebs if we so desire. Grocery shopping? Yeah, right. I already got a six-pack in the fridge—I'm good to go. They always put ketchup and salt in the takeout bag anyway—why do I need groceries? If we waited until marriage before we found these things out about ourselves, we'd hurt at least two people—her and us. A trial run is a very good thing for men who still aren't sure.

It also works the other way around—the woman might trip on you when you insist on her calling when she's going to be late or hang out with her friends instead of coming straight home. My wife and I actually had a few of these issues to work out when we first started living together (remember, honey?). Women also get used to a certain amount of carefree living. And what if homegirl turns out to be a slob and you're Mr. Neat Freak? Something and somebody will have to give. Who's it gonna be? Maybe you can stand to see her entire wardrobe spread across the apartment, or maybe you can't. (You can't possibly think I'm talking about you, right, wifey dear? Don't be ridiculous. I said ENTIRE wardrobe, not half of it.) Cohabitation will give you your answer.

As for monogamy, cohabitation might actually be helpful for some brothers. Now you no longer have an empty apartment to cheat in. You have someone checking on your whereabouts with much more regularity. Someone with the nose of a bloodhound is going to be sniffing around your clothes when you walk into the house. You have to badly want to cheat, I mean it has to be at the top of your list of priorities, right up there with tax shelters in importance, for you to get away with it on a continual basis. This thought remains in the back of your head at all times, serving as a leash that yanks you backwards or closes around your throat if you take even a step in the direction of the big butt in the miniskirt or the secretary you've renamed Miss Cleavage. For those brothers out there worried about whether they can keep it strapped down, perhaps the restrictions of cohabitation are just what the doctor ordered. Think of your new housemate as inoculation for a cheating heart.

Oh, one more thing. Your rent and household expenses are now sliced in half. That's like having your salary doubled. Mo' money, mo' money, mo' money. Not much bad in that.

If you catch your man cheating while you're cohabiting, are you more or less likely to end the relationship than if you caught him while you were married?

From a Sistah
Like, which way would you prefer? Lorena Bobbitt real slow-like, or Lorena Bobbitt quick and clean? Either way, it . . . er, I mean, you—yeah, you—are going to get cut off.

Cheating on a sistah while you two are living together? That's the quick-and-clean Bobbitt. We adore you, and emotionally, it's like we're married—sans the ring and wedding cake. But it's much easier to step with simply a broken heart and a broken lease when there's no marriage certificate standing in the way.

Don't get me wrong: We put high value on living with someone. You aren't just a roommate—you're a best friend, you're a lover, you're a partner in finances, you're the other half—and we take the relationship seriously. And when we sign that lease together, it means that we've made the commitment to respect each other to the fullest, and to respect equally the sanctity of this relationship, as we are one step away from the next logical destination—marriage. Living together is the trial run.

And you would fail the test miserably if I found out you were dipping in someone else's cookie jar. We would take it as a serious sign that things would only get worse—definitely not better—if we married your ass. So, no matter how painful it may be emotionally, you're going to get Bobbitted, quick, fast and in a hurry.

Marriage? Well, that's a whole 'nother story. You're talking about a relationship that's reached its height. This is no longer a lease, it's a mortgage. It's no longer my stereo from college—it's our stereo we bought together. It may no longer be just the two of us—it could very well be you, me and the kids.

Simply put: The stakes are higher.

The fact of the matter is that you don't just walk away from marriage. You don't just give another woman that much dap that she can sleep with your man and take all of your shit with her. And you certainly don't let homeboy off so easy by simply telling him to pack up his stuff and get out.

(Ooh—I can hear the finger-snapping and feel the neck-rolling from the sistah girls as I write this—but I'm trying to be honest here. I think it's easy for us sistahs to proudly proclaim that any man who betrayed them with adultery would just be gone. If she's being honest with herself, she knows that when it comes to marriage, it's just not that simple—even though it's the most miserable thing her soulmate could ever do to her.)

That's not to say that we won't want to Bobbitt you; it would hurt like hell and we would make you suffer like you've never suffered before—because we, too, would be suffering. It's the ultimate betrayal, adultery, and it's not an easy one to get over. In fact, we may never get over it, which gets me back to the Bobbitt slow-like torture. That's the one where you spend the rest of the marriage trying to make it up to me, and then, eventually, I crack under the pressure of wondering whether or not it's going to happen again, and leave yo' ass anyway.

Either way, you've been Bobbitted.

Refined or Freaky?

From a Sistah

Every sistah with a bit of sense knows that freaks don't get invited to his mama's dinner table—at least, that's what our mamas told us. (For those of us whose moms were in denial and refused to talk about that kinda stuff, it's pretty much an unwritten rule you learn from experience: You want the ring, you DO NOT ask him on the first date if his chandelier will hold you—period.)

Nobody put it better than comedian Chris Rock when he joked that while men know they can't throw out any of that "weak" stuff on their first groove on with a woman, sistahs know they have to "ration" out the good stuff over time.

That means you sleep with him after a respectable dating period—never on the first date. The number of positions you can maneuver are limited to just a few until he's comfortable enough to think he taught you the new ones you slipped in on him. That means you leave the toys and dirty talk at home.

That means you become the good girl he can put on the pedestal—the one the brother could envision having his babies and growing old with and stuff, right?

Well, we sistahs are confused, then.

We don't quite get how the women who are freaks seem to get all the play. Don't front: We can't count how many brothers have gotten caught out there in the back seat with Sheila—which wouldn't have been a bad thing if homeboy's wife's name wasn't Jane. You know the type: They get the good-girl wife and keep a few freaks on the side.

She walks up into the club with pleather, spikes and a weave, and the brothers are jockin' her like a doggie does a juicy ham bone.

She turns him out tonight—he's coming back for more tomorrow, Monday, Wednesday, March, April, August, and any other day that's not a holiday because, of course, he will be home with the good girl for Christmas, Thanksgiving, Valentine's Day and every other holiday that requires a boyfriend's presence.

And therein lies the rub.

We hit you with the missionary—we're sentenced to a turn on the good-girl pedestal and a lot of lonely Saturday nights. We hit you with more positions than the *Kama Sutra,* we get every Saturday night—which is a great thing—but no dinner at Mama's, right?

Help us out: If we're looking for the permanent hookup, should we be refined or freaky?

From a Brother
You should be a refined freak. That means to wield the freakiness with the precision of a surgeon's blade.

First, let me point out that there are two types of freaks: the public freak and the private freak. The public freak loudly—emphasis on *loud*—announces to the world that she's a highly sexual being and willingly displays all the requisite physical attributes. Her style of dress leaves nothing to the imagination and would attract the vice squad if she lingered too long at an intersection. She burns candles every night to pay homage to the inventor of Spandex.

The private freak appears on the surface to be as refined and normal as your high school English teacher, but when the door closes and the lights go down (actually, she sometimes leaves the lights on), she transmutes into Vanessa Del Rio. She's afraid of nothing; she'll try anything; she's the closest thing to insatiable you'll ever meet. In fact, she kinda scares you a little.

The public freak is going to attract our attention like a cat to a mouse. In fact, even after the public freak has passed out of our line of sight, we may never forget her. We might spend quite a few of our waking hours thinking about her. When we fall asleep, her face and form will likely figure prominently in those dreams that still occasionally result in embarrassing emissions. Virtually everything about her has a magical effect on our lower appendage.

But you'd have to put a gun to our head before we'd let anybody see us with her. If we get a chance with her, we'll make sure it happens either well after the sun has descended into the horizon or in a place far enough from our regular haunts that we feel incognito. And if the stuff is so good that we can't stay away, we'll buy her gifts and bring her expensive takeout to assuage the guilt we feel from the knowledge that we'd give up a limb before we'd take her home to meet Mom. Speaking of the goodness of her "stuff," I should note that her public display has lifted our expectations incredibly high. We're anticipating that she will show us things we didn't think we'd ever see if we weren't willing to pay for it. Unless she's been training with the aforementioned Miss Del Rio, she's likely to leave us disappointed.

The private freak is, as one of my friends used to say, "a whole 'nother story." There's nothing quite so thrilling as finding out that that classy, refined lady who knew exactly which fork to use turns into a nasty tigress in the bedroom. It'd be like if somebody told you that chocolate fudge could prolong your life—not only mind-blowingly delectable, but good for you, too. Most of us are taught to not expect such miracles. A private freak is like a big, cold glass of lemonade on a steamy summer afternoon, like a warm bath after a strenuous workout. She is an introduction to perfection. We would die for her.

But she must be exceedingly careful in revealing her freakiness. She must walk a terribly fine line. What we're looking for is sexual curiosity and a willingness to try anything. However, we don't want to get the impression that she's already DONE everything. Because then a voice in the back of our head starts suggesting that maybe she's also done EVERYBODY. In our manual, too much sexual expertise is a red flag, a warning light, a flashing neon sign. It makes us nervous.

If you are in possession of a well-stocked bag of toys, hide it at the back of that overburdened closet, far from our line of sight. 'Cause once we see that, though our eyes might light up and our pencil harden instantly, that bag is going to plague us forever. My suggestion to you is to unveil the contents of the bag one by one, with weeks and even months between unveilings, and each time give us the impression that the toy is something you just bought specifically for our pleasure and entertainment. Because if we know that dildo has been clutched by some other brother, or that velvet rope has been tied around somebody else's wrists, we're going to have second and third and fourth thoughts about a future with you.

In the end, what we want is this: a nasty, imaginative sex goddess who also happens to be a virgin.

Ridiculous. Impossible. Illogical. Yet, still within your reach. For this discussion, *virgin* means all your previous lovers are vague and unidentifiable in name and number. Because a brother's worst nightmare is to profess his undying love for you, to slide that engagement ring on your finger, to introduce you to all the friends and relatives, then find out all his boys and his boys' boys are snickering behind his back because they too have tasted the goodies and played with the toys.

So the private freak is a gift from the heavens, but only if she doesn't give us the clear impression that her freakiness is the result of indiscriminate coupling and frequent practice. The public freak is exciting as hell—but only appropriate on the down low, in the late hours.

I do wonder, though, whether we have any options at our disposal to turn our refined lady into a private freak. **If we start**

asking you to do freak-like things, will we find ourselves sleeping in the hallway with Rover?

From a Sistah

Pull out a whip unexpectedly, and you're going to get your feelings hurt—and a few other things by the time the cops finish with you.

Now, don't get us wrong: We do want you to hit the home run—to knock it, so to speak, out of the box. We do not want psycho-sex-maniac-man pouring hot wax on our prone, tied bodies—unless we ask for it, thank you. And guaranteed, we sistahs won't be asking for that the first time we sleep with you—at least not those of us who are in this with you for more than just one night. See, on the first few times around, we're just as unsure about our sexual roles as we're sure you men are. We're not quite sure how you will respond to our bodies, whether you'll like our techniques, or—the big one—whether what we're doing with you will mean our relationship is through, that you've gotten what you wanted and tomorrow you will be gone. So while all of this tension is coursing through our minds, the last thing we need is for you to pull out the blindfold.

That's not to say we won't appreciate a little freakiness later on down the road. It should not, however, come before we are ready. It's all about our comfort level. On your first night together, the sistah may not be comfortable taking off her clothes in front of you or having sex with the lights on. By the third time you two are together, she may be comfortable having sex with you by candlelight. By the fifth tryst, she may be comfortable experimenting a little more—perhaps during a morning shower or a late-night bubble bath. By the tenth liason, she may be thinking you're Brother Mr. Right—and we all know that the right one can get you to doing things you never dreamed you'd do, stuff that'd make your daddy disown you—things that would have you sitting in church and silently asking the Lord for forgiveness.

Then again, maybe she won't be into any of this.

But you'll never find out unless you know how comfortable she is with it, and you'll only know how comfortable she is with it if you ask. Communication, as with all things, is of the utmost importance here.

When's a good time to ask? When she's no longer afraid that you'll be turned off by her eye boogers and bad morning breath. If she's not getting up an hour before you do to get her face together, then she's comfortable around you, and you, too, should feel more comfortable asking.

Of course, it wouldn't be fair if we simply left all the responsibility in your hands. We sistahs could stand a few lessons in how to speak up when it comes to bedroom matters, too. We, after all, also want to be pleased, don't we? Gone are the days when we just lay there and take whatever stuff brothers throw our way, and then we happily go on about our business unsatisfied but glad that at least he got what he wanted. Problem is that not too many of us sistahs are secure in asking for what we want—and others are good at barking orders and still not getting what they want.

So our question is: How aggressive should we be in asking you for sexual satisfaction?

From a Brother

Too much aggression is never good, whether we're talking lovers or tax accountants. An aggressive woman is scary as hell.

As we turn off the lights and start the intimacy dance, we don't want to feel undue pressure. The pressure we place on ourselves produces enough anxiety—Will she think I'm adequate? Will all the equipment respond when called on? Is my deodorant still working?—without any added stress from a demanding woman who is barking orders like a gym teacher. No brother wants all that. We want to be told gently and affectionately where to go and what to do if she has somehow gotten the idea that we'd be unlikely to make it there on our own. This should come in the form of soft suggestions, maybe whispered sexily in our ear. In the throes of ecstasy we don't mind hearing some loudly expressed demands or affirmations of our skills, but reprimands or scolds should wait until later.

One thing Jimmy definitely doesn't appreciate is being yelled at. Or threatened. Or ordered to perform. He doesn't listen when we do it, so he certainly wouldn't be inclined to obey a voice that hasn't been there with him throughout the years, stroking him affectionately when he was down and lonely, protecting him from harm when danger menaced. Jimmy can be one of the most temperamental creatures on earth. And we never know when he's going to emerge in one of his moods. So we try to treat him gingerly, feed him well and give him as much warm company as he deserves.

Though many men may occasionally wonder what an evening with such famously aggressive temptresses as Madonna or Lil' Kim would consist of, the actual thought of being alone with them scares the hell out of many of us. These women aren't afraid to screech to the world what they want and how they want it. What would they do if our performance wasn't quite up to their standards? It's almost frightening enough to make me shudder. We might wind up in a song, our name attached to an adjective that rhymes with "rich." What would our boys say?

At this point, we feel the need to discuss a topic on which we both agree: Safe Sex. In the realm of relationships and love-making in the black community, no discussion is more important.

Though African Americans make up 13 percent of the U.S. population, we account for approximately 57 percent of all new HIV infections and nearly half of all AIDS cases, according to recent figures compiled by the Centers for Disease Control and Prevention. AIDS remains the leading cause of death among black people age twenty-five to forty-four. In other words, our community is ground zero in the war against AIDS, and we desperately need to start educating and cherishing each other.

Whose responsibility is it to make sure both partners are protected, the man's or the woman's?

The easy answer is that it's the responsibility of both the man and the woman, but in the heated, whispered moments of pre-sex intimacy, the logistics can be daunting—particularly with a new partner. Should I stop him? Will she be upset if I zip up my pants and run to the drugstore—and will she still be in the mood when I come back? These are rational questions that run through our heads.

If the use of a condom becomes the across-the-board expectation in all of our sexual encounters, black women will no longer have to worry about whether a dude will be offended when she politely tells him to slip on the contraceptive—and black men will be sure never to be caught without one. This sexual rights movement needs to start gaining some momentum. But joining the movement is on you—you're not likely going to look up from between the sheets one night to find Rosa Parks standing over your bed handing you a condom.

The only reason condom talk is still dicey for some couples and there are still some black men out there who might be offended by the idea of a condom is because the sex education in our community has been much too passive and limited. Some of us just don't know. But the others, the ones who are aware of the dangers of HIV infection and still don't seek protection 100 percent of the time, are playing Russian roulette with not only their own lives but the lives of future sex partners and unborn children.

One final word: For those who claim that using a condom just "doesn't feel as good," get over it. It feels good enough to get the job done. As far as we know, there are no documented cases of men who failed to achieve orgasm because sex with a condom just wasn't satisfying enough.

Couples and Conflict: How Do We Deal?

From a Sistah

We don't exactly get off on getting mad, but hey—tick us off, and we have no other choice but to take it there. And we are good at keeping it there until we feel the situation is resolved, thank you.

Of course, that could take anywhere from five minutes to five hours to five days to forever—depending on your response. All too often, that response is the same: You all just drop it. And when you do that, we want to blow up the argument like the World Trade Center.

Why? Because we want to resolve whatever it is that's the source of the argument. We want to talk about it, air our feelings, let you know we didn't appreciate whatever atrocity—big or small—you've committed against us. It could be as simple as you leaving the toilet seat up—again—or as complicated as our holding you accountable for forgetting to pick up the kids from soccer practice—again. The simple fact is that we want to discuss what happened, tell you how mad or perturbed we are with your behavior and its consequences, and discuss it some more—until we're satisfied that you get it. And getting it means you sympathize with our plight, pontificate on why you committed whatever transgression you committed, and express sincere and prolonged remorse, until we feel you are truly suffering and sorry. In the cases where you're not wrong and we recognize this, we still want you to argue— because we feel like you should let us know what's on your mind and defend yourself from our wrongful attack.

That's right, I'm admitting it: A good deal of us are emotional, and we need to express it, particularly in situations where there is conflict. It has nothing to do with PMS, nothing to do with brattiness or divadom. It's our need and desire for expression. And we get downright frustrated when you all don't respond in the same exact way, because we feel like you're holding back.

Admittedly, some of us are used to you all saying a simple "I'm sorry" and moving on as if everything is hunky-freakin'-dory. It takes a certain amount of resolve to do that. But the vast majority of us down here on sistah-girl earth want to know this: **When it comes to conflict, why don't you all argue?**

From a Brother

Because we want as little fuss as possible, that's why. We won't compromise all our principles and beliefs for a little peace and quiet—just most of them. We don't want to sweat the small stuff— and, to quote a popular book, it's all small stuff.

It's always easier to let the woman win, or at least to let her think she's won, than to keep the fuss going. That doesn't mean we've given up all power to the woman or that we don't care about anything. We care a great deal. But our days and nights are much more pleasant if our woman isn't mad at us. If we deploy our weapons and win the argument, usually we've actually lost the war because the things that are important to us—peace and quiet; a smile from our lady; a little nookie—are denied until the cold front blows over. There are very few arguments worth all that.

Of course, if we felt the woman could lose and then not walk around with a stank attitude, we probably would argue a little more. But our experience tells us that the ammunition we would need to summon in order to win—namely, recalling examples of when you screwed up, or you forgot our birthday, or you were engrossed in that Maxwell video and not listening, or you acted like you didn't care—would make you very unhappy. An unhappy woman in our household is not pleasant. To avoid all that, we are usually quite willing to throw the game.

This is behavior we learn from an early age hanging out with our boys. Yeah, we might play the dozens and try to slice and dice our dearest homeboys over their wardrobe or jump shot or lack of dancing skills, but somehow things are usually kept light and humorous. We try not to let the dissing creep too close to home, because true feelings get hurt and someone wants to fight. So we quickly learn the art of insult without hurt, or dis without damage. In other words, these aren't real arguments that we've learned to engage in—they're more like play-fighting, that slap-

slap that black men like to engage in on street corners or courtyard sidelines.

Fast-forward to adulthood and our relationships with our women. As you have stated in your question, you all don't mind arguing one bit. Some of you might even enjoy it a little sometimes, or so it seems. You surely haven't learned to do the slap-slap play-fighting with your girls—otherwise, y'all wouldn't be mad at each other every other week. So verbal encounters are the real thing, slash-and-burn, win at all costs. We learn this very quickly; we learn to avoid it at all costs. We've always been afraid of these real arguments, the ones with consequences. We want play-fighting or nothing. You come at us with guns blazing, looking for a standoff at the O.K. Corral at noon—we scurry away to look for cover underneath the nearest wagon.

Also, as I've said elsewhere, we rarely remember enough really good stuff to win these arguments about past behavior anyway. Our women seem to be keeping a scorecard somewhere—we never see you actually pull out a notebook or a laptop, but somewhere you're keeping a running tab of our transgressions that pops up in your short-term memory whenever needed, like one of those dialog boxes in a Windows program. Our hard drive just doesn't seem capable of storing the same amount of data. You might try suggesting that we have much less data to work with—that is, you commit far fewer transgressions—but I disagree. I think you guys mess up just as much—I just can't remember when, that's all.

We'd be more willing to engage in verbal duels with you if we didn't think they'd all end so badly. If they were more like the relationships we maintain with our boys, the no-consequence square-offs, perhaps we wouldn't be so afraid of them. But as things are now, rarely are these verbal duels worth it to us. We gain nothing from them but hurt feelings and silent households. And though we sometimes don't pretend to want to spend all night talking to you, there's nothing worse than walking around a cold, hostile house where the only rise we get from you is an occasional growl or icy stare—when you bother to even acknowledge our presence. You remember those nights, right, dear? My butt is still frostbitten from the last icy stare I got from you. Why would we willingly go looking for any more of those?

Perhaps we could agree either to hire a referee to work our arguments, or we could sign a contract beforehand that no one is going to resort to the silent treatment if things get too heated. The contract could stipulate in no uncertain terms that we still love each other no matter what. I know that sounds next to impossible, but that may be the only thing that'll draw us out. Otherwise, argument is not worth the risk; we'd rather just shut it down and throw in the quick towel.

If we really did argue with you more, wouldn't it make us look too belligerent and scary? Do you really want a man who'd rather have argument than peace in his household?

From a Sistah

We want peace in the household, too—but we'd much rather work out our problem by talking it through than having you drop the issue at hand and act as if everything is fine and freakin' dandy.

Nobody's telling you to be belligerent and scary; the last thing a sistah wants is a man who is bigger and stronger getting in her face, acting like he's going to mete out some physical abuse to make his point. We don't respond very well to bullies—particularly ones we love.

We do, however, respond very well when a brother makes his point—or at least stands up for himself.

There is nothing more annoying on this earth than getting into a disagreement with someone and, in the midst of trying to make a point, the other person just cedes the argument and walks away. We're just sort of left standing there, brewing, knowing that even though you're making it seem like we won the argument, we really didn't—because you still have issues that you need addressed, but you won't share them with us.

It's not that we want you to put your dukes up; it's that we want to understand why you disagree with our thinking—and we want to understand why you think the way you do. And it's impossible to figure any of that out when the person in question isn't willing to reveal any of it.

We are the ones in your life. We marry you, we sleep with you, we bear your children, we go through good times and some bad times, too. We share our dreams with you—and we suffer through and make it out of a few nightmares with you by our side. So why does that sharing have to stop when we're in the middle of a not-so-pleasant experience?

Our wish is that it doesn't stop there. Arguing is a part of cleansing; in a weird way, I think it keeps us healthy—lets us know where we stand, what buttons not to push, which bridges not to cross, or burn down, for that matter. It's our way of finding out more about you—understanding you—and getting some nastiness out of our system so that we can get back to the business of loving.

All of that can be done without you getting belligerent and scary—and certainly without ending the peace in the household. If it's a healthy relationship, arguments are just something to get over, not a permanent roadblock.

Naturally, it's not always pretty or easy to deal with. We can be a bit belligerent and scary in other ways. My personal favorite is the silent treatment—doled out carefully and succinctly when my man gets on my damn nerves. He hates it, but on occasion it's extremely effective. There are times, though, when I and other sistahs tend to drag out an argument and its aftermath a tad bit too long. **How long do we have to put you through it before we absolutely piss you off and threaten the relationship?**

From a Brother

The silent treatment is infuriating. It drives us insane. Perhaps that's why you resort to it to drive your point home. But once it moves into its third day, I think the point has been made a hundredfold. At that juncture, I start wondering if maybe you wouldn't rather I go somewhere else.

Unless that's your wish—to drive your man out of the house—I would suggest that you start talking before your head has hit the pillow for a third night in a row with no word being uttered to the dude on the other side. No "good night" or even "kiss my ass, Negro." A bar, or worse, starts looking pretty good to us when compared to the silent treatment at home. We start thinking we even have justification for staying out all night or going to a booty bar with the boys and getting sloppy drunk. Unless it's your wish to send your man into the lapdance of another woman, a third day would not be advisable.

After a third day, we also start to develop some substantial anger of our own. We start thinking that our offense couldn't have been THAT egregious; we complain to ourselves that we aren't being treated fairly. We start feeling sorry for ourselves and holding you responsible for it all. And our anger isn't likely to evaporate as soon as you throw a smile in our direction. We might decide we want to hold on to it for a while. So then what do we have? Two adults engaging in a childlike dance of mutual resentment and anger, all over some disagreement that has already faded into the woodwork.

The last thing you want to do is give your man reason to believe he is being wronged at home and that he has been granted justification for running out there and doing all the things he's normally scared to death to even try. He might want to use your anger as a Get Your Rocks Off Free card. That could lead to unimaginable trouble for both of you. Holding on to your anger surely can't be worth that kind of pain. Let it go.

Getting Serious About Getting Serious

From a Sistah

See, I thought I was the one. We'd been hanging tough—doing the movies on Fridays, dinner on Sundays, each other on at least every third night. Even caught you up in my kitchen one morning, cooking pancakes, chile. Had the fresh orange juice going, some eggs and sausage on the side, and a rose in a vase, sitting on the table, right next to my plate, which was waiting for me when I came downstairs.

And we've been at this for a while, right? We've talked about our dreams, had some really great times together, displayed our inhibitions—perhaps even gotten over a few because of each other. I've shown you my vulnerable sides, and made sure to let you know I'm not a punk, either—and you've shown me all the respect due a woman whom you highly regard.

I'm getting girlfriend treatment, and basically I'm thinking—"Oh yeah, he's mine."

If that ain't serious, then what is?

I mean, we sistahs aren't trying to go out with a guy three nights a week or sleep with him twice a week if there isn't something more to this relationship than a buddy-buddy/just-kickin' thang. And you know damn well we wouldn't be cooking for your behind if we didn't think you weren't a potential Brother Mr. Right.

So we take the dates, the flowers, the cooking and the good stuff as a sign that over these past four months you've caught that feeling—the one that regulates your "I Gotta Have Her" button. We're figuring you're trying to make us yours.

And then the beeper goes off. Or the late-night/hushed-talk phone call comes—the one that has a suspicious booty-call tinge to it. Or you tell me that you can't take me out this Friday because you need to "handle some business."

And I get to wondering—"I know I didn't start out the only one, but damn, I thought we were *kickin'* it."

Then, when I start inquiring about some status, I get, "Babe. This ain't no love thang. You not getting all soft on me now, are ya? I mean, we kickin it, but we not *kickin'* it, right?"

Then I realize that Shaniqua, or Debbie, or Barb or Cathy or Carol, can come strolling down the street at any time and get some play with you because, hey—I'm not your girlfriend. We're just kickin' it. Both you and I are free to see other people—and at least one of us is, even though the other one—that would be me—isn't necessarily pleased about it. In fact, I'm damn bothered, because I know I didn't just sit here and wine and dine and romance and start falling in love with you over the past four months for nothing. I mean, I want you to be my man, and that can't happen if I'm still standing on the I-got-to-share-time-with-Shaniqua-Debbie-Barbara-Cathy-Carol line. And you know what? I don't want to step; I want *them* to get off—and I want you to recognize that what we have here is something special. I mean, you treat it like it is when you're around me, right? Then why can't you treat it that way when you're not standing in my face? Obviously, that can't happen if you're dating other people.

Or maybe you're not dating someone else. Maybe you approach exclusivity in a relationship like I do yearly trips to the dentist: You just don't wanna go there.

We know pretty soon in a relationship whether we want a guy to be our exclusive boyfriend. **When do you know that she's someone you want to date exclusively?**

From a Brother

There are two tracks here—the fast track and the slow track.

I will take them one at a time, starting with the fast track. With fast-track women, we know right away. Something just feels different from the outset, like she somehow crawled into our head and knows what we're thinking and what we want before we do. These women are rare. We know that. So when we stumble upon her, we want to hop on it right away—pun intended. And we want to keep her so far away from any other dude that we're tempted to lock her in our apartments so we don't have to share her with the rest of the world. That's the fast track.

With the slow-track women, things develop gradually— maybe no sparks at first, but then you start enjoying her company; maybe you start off as good friends who find each other mutually attractive, but then you stumble into a kiss and it's on. Many times these slow-track women sneak up on us without warning; other times we clearly see them coming—and we try unsuccessfully to get the hell out of the way. Relationships with slow-track women aren't necessarily doomed, but often there was a reason that it took so long for something to happen—such as your subconscious telling you, If you go there, you may live to regret it. That woman who works a few cubicles down from you is cute and quite sexy, but you find yourself frowning every time you hear her slam the phone down on clients after she's cursed them out. A voice in the back of your head is whispering loud enough for you to hear that she has some serious anger issues—but homegirl is smiling real pretty in your face, asking about your family, inviting herself to lunch with you, and next thing you know you're up in her apartment with your tongue down her throat. You still may resist, but then perhaps she whips it on you a few times and you start thinking, Damn, this is pretty good. I like this a lot. I want this as much as possible. You start to date exclusively, you smile when she whips it on you . . . then, as the frying pan is whizzing toward your head, you ask yourself why you didn't listen to the damn voice.

Fast-track women are addictive, exhilarating, intoxicating. Right away you never want them to leave your side. She steps into your car for the first time, hears the sweet tones of Dianne Reeves cooing from the speakers, and tells you Dianne has long been her favorite singer. You walk into her apartment—and she has the same Gauguin print above her sofa that is hanging in your bedroom. The two of you glide into the bedroom for the first time and you're shocked to discover that not only do you share the same beloved positions, you fit together like a hand in glove. In other words, that same voice in the back of your head starts whispering that you just may have stumbled upon your soulmate—an occurrence only a tiny proportion of us ever experiences.

I've had fast-track and I've had slow-track; the things that prevented me from diving headfirst into the slow-track relationships were usually the things that eventually ended them. In the beginning she seems a little evil; in the end she's real evil. In the beginning she was kinda dumb; in the end she's impossibly stupid. Our instincts are vital and purposeful here; they're trying to send us signals. Many of us turn a blind eye and deaf ear, seduced by the curve of the booty or the slant of the eyes. We ought to be listening to those instincts more often. We'd be doing ourselves and the lady a favor by staying out of those pairings that will inflict pain on all involved parties.

Then there's the sex. As we all well know, sex gets us brothers into all manner of foul situations. The non-thinking little head. How many times have we heard the little head cursed to no end, or cursed him ourselves? Just as the little head will lead us to offer rides to women named Divine standing at the intersection in microminis at 2:00 A.M., or to spend too much time with overly friendly interns wearing berets and kneepads, it'll also drag us into ill-advised relationships with women that will only cause us terrific anguish. If the sex is good, consistent and has been somewhat hard to come by lately, the bachelor can convince himself of such utter love and devotion that he might even ignore the way his stomach roils when he wakes up in the morning and realizes she's still there, her split ends breaking off all over the pillowcase, the covers all bunched up around her too-comfortable form. But we can ignore it for only so long. Eventually, the big head takes over and reminds us that this woman has nothing to offer besides an especially agile receptacle for our flowing passion.

But sometimes the big head is sleeping, almost as if the little head has some type of hypnotic power. One of these days, I believe, biologists are going to announce that they've discovered a powerful but undetectable scent emitted from the little head that freezes all thought processes in the big head and lulls the male into becoming a walking, talking, brainless erection. It will explain a whole lot of male behavior. Drug companies will make ever-more billions selling a lotion that overwhelms the undetectable scent. With a few strokes of lotion, males will be freed from the penis prison that has kept us chained, stupid and vulnerable for thousands of years.

Can women sense when a man is reluctant to enter an exclusive relationship, even if he decides to go ahead and do it?

From a Sistah

Yup, but we'll just jump right into the relationship anyway because a he-don't-really-wanna-be-here-but-he's-here-right-now relationship is better than no relationship at all to too many of us sistahs.

Make no mistake about it: We can smell it a mile away—and it's most apparent not in what you do, but what you don't do for our relationship.

Take my college girlfriend (who shall remain nameless because this scenario is too raw and painful for her to see her name attached to it in print) and her now-ex-boyfriend (I shall call him Manchild, because that's what he is). Their relationship had all the trappings of a disaster—even Stevie Wonder could see that. About six years after we all graduated from college, she reacquainted herself with Manchild, whom we'd both known as a playa-from-the-Himalayas back at school. She thought he'd grown up by now, seeing as we were adults and not freshmen running around boning everything in sight just because—and he'd sort of displayed that he had. He was a gentleman now—someone had cut his hair, dressed him up and given him a breath mint—but he was still a bow-wow—you could smell it behind his ears. He romanced her, wined and dined her, turned her out, basically—and she wholeheartedly fell for him hook, line and sinker.

Didn't matter to her that homeboy was a two-time divorcé (already—even though we hadn't even gotten on our first marriage yet) and was apparently dating a bevy of women besides her. Didn't matter that they paged, called and e-mailed him on the regular, and that he wasn't particularly adept at playing it off or hiding them. Didn't matter that even on some special occasions, like birthdays, Christmas or whatever, she'd search for reasons to believe him when he said, "I just want to spend time alone, and be with myself on this special day, and connect with the Creator."

He was becoming one all right—with another woman. And my girl had even found out about a few of them, too. One who lived down the street from his apartment and whom he claimed was "just a friend" even told my girl that they had a thing going on. My girl's response? She cursed out the woman, withheld the nookie from her man for, like, a week, and then resumed the relationship like everything was back to normal. Then she found out a few months later that there was another woman—an acquaintance of hers, no less—who had made plans to take her man out on the same weekend that my girl was planning a special somethin' somethin' for him. When Manchild abruptly changed up on his plans, my girl got suspicious and listened to his answering machine, only to find a message from the acquaintance telling Manchild that she "just couldn't wait for our trip to the country this weekend."

My girlfriend yelled at him, screamed on him, hung the phone up in his face and vowed she'd never, ever trust or date him again—and we were all, like, "Damn, it's about time she got it." See, the two failed marriages should have been a sign—a little one, but a sign nonetheless—as it told her that he'd had problems with commitment. But any sane, rational, sweet person like my girlfriend would easily overlook that, because those two women were not her. She was different, or so she thought, and their relationship wouldn't suffer the failure that his other two did.

The second sign that he wasn't ready for a serious commited relationship should have been his constant connection with other women. He'd dismissed it to her by saying they were just his friends, but clearly she was uncomfortable with his so-called friendships, enough to suspect that she wasn't the only one in his life. But she let it go—let her heart trust that he was telling the truth, even though her brain told her the exact opposite.

The third sign that she ignored came straight from the horse's mouth. Manchild was damn-near schizophrenic. The sistahs know the type. One day he'd tell her he wanted to get married, the next day he'd say he wasn't sure if he'd ever see himself in a stable, committed relationship because he wasn't "ready" to go there just yet. He'd tell her that they should think about starting a family one day, and the next week homeboy was saying he didn't want kids because he was afraid he wouldn't be a good father. He'd go on a trip and tell her he'd miss her while he was gone, and then she wouldn't hear from him the entire time he'd be on the road. Then he would come back home with a ton of gifts to prove, "I was thinking about you the whole time, babe."

To a Monday-morning quarterback, it was pretty obvious that homeboy was playing the mess out of sistah-girl. He wasn't looking to get serious about her relationship any more than the man on the moon. But when you're in it, you want the man, not the heartache that comes with having to break up with him and then facing a multitude of lonely weekends alone. We sistahs try entirely too hard to make it work, which isn't a bad thing if the relationship is worth it and he's committed to helping make it work. But if it's one-sided, there really is no more point to it, other than being able to say, "I got a man."

We're hooked on that "I Got a Man" syndrome—and no matter how terrible the disease, we'll let him stick to us like a bad rash rather than rub some calamine lotion on his butt and make him disappear.

Not all of us are like this, but too many of us are. We just have a knack for knowing what we want up front, and doing everything within our power to make it work. It doesn't take forever for us to decide—and we certainly aren't accustomed to dating 20 guys at the same time before we decide which one would be the best for us (although I propose that it would be great if we did, as we'd weed out the losers without wasting too much of our time). You all don't seem to operate the way we do, though. It almost seems as if you guys employ the date-as-many-as-you-can approach before you get to the point where you feel comfortable settling down with just one. We want to know how we can be that "one."

What signs should I look for to tell me you're not headed in that direction?

From a Brother

Yeah, some of us just aren't ready yet. Some of us might not even be close to ready. But that doesn't mean we don't like having you around. We don't want you to go anywhere—we like you a lot. Really. We're just wanting to fix up our credit . . . get a new car first . . . get a new apartment first . . . get a new job first . . . get our teeth fixed first . . . you get the idea.

So I have provided yet another service for the sistahs. The following are some things to look for that should cause lights to start flashing in a sistah's head, telling her the man just ain't ready:

- His hand flies to his throat and he has difficulty breathing every time you pass by a jewelry store at the mall.
- He doesn't even know how to spell the word m-a-r-i-a-g-g-e.
- He gets pissed off when you wear white.

• He claims you shouldn't leave any clothes at his place 'cause he has very aggressive moths—that's why he ain't hardly bought no clothes.

• He plays the *Living Single* theme song—the one with Queen Latifah blowing—on the CD player in his ride.

• The local booty bar sends overdue notices to his house because he hasn't paid his running tab.

• He tells you he promised himself he wouldn't make any major life decisions until the Knicks won another NBA championship.

• After his best friend got married, he locked himself up in his apartment for a week and refused to answer the phone.

• He says he's just trying to protect you from his mother— she thinks no girl is good enough for little Tyrone.

The Big "C" : The Ring, the Ceremony, Forever

From a Sistah

No, see, you don't understand. We want the ring. We may not just come right out and say it, we may not make it immediately clear from the getty-up (well, some of us just might), but we want to get married—particularly if we've been dating for some time now. It's just logical: we meet, we date, we date exclusively, we get hitched. Simple as that.

For us, at least.

You guys? Well, that's a whole different bag. We sistahs get the distinct impression that you'd rather cross a pit of burning hot coals, with needles stuck in your eyes, butt-naked, in full makeup and a RuPaul wig on national television—preferably in the NBC Thursday-evening 9:00 P.M.-post–Seinfeld slot—with your mama sitting in the center of the front row of the studio audience, rather than work your lips to ask us to marry you. You all get the hives when we look like we're about to bring it up, and start stuttering like baleep, baleep, Pa-pa-porky the Pi-pi-pig when we ask you to discuss your intentions.

"I mean, we've been dating for five years now," the sistah says. "I love you, you know that, and you say you love me. What's wrong with making it official?"

"We-we-well, baby—everything's ga-ga-good between us. You don't na-ne-need a ma-ma-ma—um—piece of paper to confirm my love for you."

And why not? There is so much more security in the relationship when you've got the papers. It's like, we've stood before God and said that we will be faithful and true and love each other come what may, and here's the certificate and the ring to symbolize that vow of commitment.

Then there's the kid thing—with the two of us being the parents in a traditional household. Not knocking the single-parent thing, or the live-in thing, for that matter. In fact, I fully advocate the latter, as it's the only possible way, I think, that two people can truly get to know each other before they take such a huge step into the commitment of marriage. But it's got to come to the marriage eventually, or it's like this relationship isn't official. It makes it a helluva lot easier to walk away from a relationship. Marriage? Well, there's no way you can just waltz away from that. It automatically elevates our status, makes us both think and try a lot harder to patch up the not-so-good things and work even more to create better times and a stronger bond for our relationship. If you're thinking about walking away from a long-term relationship, you know all you'll have is a broken heart and a broken lease. You think about walking away from a marriage, and you come to your senses more quickly—realize that it's not so easy to walk away, that you have to try to make it stick because she is your wife, you are her husband and you told the Lord, the minister and your mama you two were in this for life.

Perhaps the scariest thing that could happen in New York recently was Mayor Rudy Giuliani's decision to let domestic partners receive benefits. The measure, geared toward homosexual couples who can't, by law, get married, allows longtime partners to receive all the benefits of a married couple, without having to tie the knot. If one has good benefits on the job, the other can be covered under that plan. If one dies, the other can inherit the deceased's apartment/house/car et al. There's one catch, though: The domestic partner rule isn't limited to homosexual couples—heterosexual couples can take advantage, too. That means that boyfriend doesn't even have to put a ring on her finger; she'll get dental, free gynecological care and a right to the apartment without him having to "suffer" being married to her. It completely goes against the whole institution of marriage—makes it easier to justify why you don't have to do it.

Figures a man came up with the idea.

You know what? We don't want lifetime playmates; we want for-real commitments, the ring, the Big C—the minister, the flower girl and the aunt singing (albeit a bit off-key) "A Ribbon in the Sky." The whole nine. And we think that you guys should feel the same way about us—particularly if we've invested a ton of time in this relationship and I love you and you claim to love me. **What's up with that? Why are brothers so afraid of the "Big C"?**

From a Brother

Well, you know what we fear, right? We fear that once we make that commitment and decide once and for all that you're the one, forever and ever, till death us do part and all that, then SHE will walk down the street, stroll right in front of our face, and smile. We'll think SHE is the most beautiful woman to walk the earth and what SHE wanted most in life was to make us hers. But no, we won't be available for SHE because we gotta stay with you or die.

Yes, of course this is stupid and childish and ridiculous. Of course you're the most beautiful woman to walk the earth and certainly if you weren't there's no reason to believe the woman who is would be smiling up in our face. Of course we gotta make decisions and then stick by them, because that's what adults do. We know all that. But then there are the sneakers.

You see, just as our lives have been carefully stage-managed by the gods of fate so that we'd one day be primed and ready for you, we have also spent the other part of our lives in search of the coolest, phattest pair of sneakers. We sauntered into Sneaker World that first time by ourselves, oh, 'bout ten, twenty, thirty years ago, our sweaty palms leaking moisture all over the $20, $50 or (if this was in the past decade) $100 balled up in our pocket. Our eyes fastened lovingly on the Havliceks or Dr. J.s or Penny Hardaways or Air Jordans in the center display. We knew this would be the shoe that would make us happy forever. Not only would we become a whirling, spinning, slam-dunking dervish on the court, but Sharon or Ayesha in the other seventh-grade class would profess her undying love for us once she caught a glimpse of the jewels on our feet. We slide them oh so carefully on our feet the next morning as we head out to school. We can just feel the eyes of the world on our feet; we know there has never been a cooler kid with a cooler shoe since man walked upright. And then disaster strikes. We're leaning against the wall before the bell, chatting with our boys, regaling them with the legend of our solo sneaker purchase, when up walks Tyrone/Raheem, sporting the newer, more expensive, oh-so-much-phatter limousine for the feet that was being sold at the newer, fancier Sneaker World at the mall where white people shop. Our friends all drift over to Tyrone/Raheem, never even giving us or our foot jewels a second glance. All those chores, all that time watching the jar fill up, all that anticipation, comes rushing back to us, leaving a bitter taste in our mouth. It is a taste we will never forget.

Fast-forward two decades. Every time you bring up the subject of long-term, forever-type commitment, we start tasting a bit terness in our mouths. We blink rapidly, we shake our heads furiously, we take a few deep breaths. Still, we can't get rid of the taste. It won't go away. The sneakers.

How long into the relationship do you start looking at us cross-eyed if we haven't broached the subject of marriage or given you some clue that we're thinking about it?

From a Sistah

For some of us, it's immediate. We will set a deadline for ourselves and cut your black butt off quicker than the jury freed O.J. if you're just sort of carrying on with no firm commitment coming down the pike. Ain't nobody trying to turn gray waiting for you to get your stuff together.

I have a girlfriend who lets guys know up front that she's looking for a husband, and that if he's not looking for a long-term commitment within their first two years of dating, she's not even trying to stick around. She has, after all, a wedding to plan.

For a lot of others, though, it's ridiculously too long. I'd heard some horror stories out on the road that plain turned my stomach—stories about sistahs who'd been in relationships with men for near-lifetimes, y'all, and were still waiting, hoping, praying and begging for that ring. One woman from the D.C. area told me that her brother had this one girl all strung out—had three kids with her, the last one born around the same time as another child homeboy had sired with some other woman he'd been dating on the side of his main squeeze. The couple, according to the *Sistahs' Rules* woman, had been together fourteen years—fourteen years, y'all—and homegirl was still talking about "I want to get married, but he says I should just sit tight—we don't need a piece of paper to prove we're together."

Right.

Of course, the logical argument here is that homegirl has invested fourteen years in this relationship—and at this point, she's probably not seeing any tangible reason why she should leave. She's got a man (kinda), a father for her three kids, and basic security, as they live together and he, no doubt, pays a sizable sum to keep the family comfortable. Why would she want to start over—give up all of that stability (if you wish to call it that) to put herself back on the market, three kids and all? It would mean that she wasted fourteen solid years of her life—and at that point, it's *easier* to keep him.

Which leads me right to my point: Too many of us figure it's easier to keep him—easier to just go on along with the program rather than to be alone. We'd just as soon settle for fourteen years of so-so commitment, half happiness, big-time disappointment with him just because we can't stand the idea of having to go it alone—as if a man somehow makes us whole. It's a serious problem. We're in an unstable, miserable relationship, it's easy to say, "Girl—you need to just walk away." But doing it isn't all that simple.

There are other sistahs who are simply content dating men—having a companion without the firm marriage commitment thing. They're older, quite set in their ways, quite used to not having to disrupt their quiet, self-centered lives to split everything down the middle with some Negro. Fine if he wants to go to the movies or the museum—out to dinner and perhaps a little sleepover afterward—but, please, no marriage, because marriage will just screw it up.

But there is no science to figuring out which one you're going to get. She may, like my girlfriend, tell you up front that if you're not in it for the commitment, get to stepping. She may let you sit up in her house for a billion years, bear your kids and never make you get out. Or she may just let you stick around for a decent amount of time without talk of "the ring," ask you what's happening if you appear to be moving just a little too slow for comfort, and book up if you don't eventually—but in a reasonable amount of time—come around.

I can tell you, however, what you can do to help it along: You can stop playing games and just get to it—tell us if you're seriously considering marrying us, or if you're just sticking around until "SHE" miraculously reveals herself to you. Of course, we could make it even easier than that, and once we figure out if we really want you, we just come on out and ask you for *your* hand in marriage. **How would you respond if we asked you to marry us?**

From a Brother

Yeah, right. Y'all can't even get up the nerve to ask a brother to dance with you. I'm supposed to believe there are sistahs out there who'd actually ask a brother for his hand in marriage? Are you also gonna slide a nice big diamond ring on my finger? Am I supposed to cry and go call my dad to share the news with him?

Most of the brothers I know would have some problems with getting a proposal from a sistah, even if they had planned on doing it themselves at some point. The circumstances of our proposal—time, place, carat size, knee or no knee, trickery or straightforward—are details that cause a great deal of stress, but it's a good stress because we retain control of the event. We can do it when we're ready to do it, how we want to do it. Sure, you ladies are put in the difficult position of having to wait . . . and wait . . . and wait . . . for us to get around to it, but the last thing you should want is for your man to feel rushed or forced into marriage, trapped into giving the answer he thinks she wants to hear. That's a recipe for disaster. When the sistah proposes to the brother, there's too great a danger that he's not going to be ready yet.

If this is a woman we are growing to love, we don't want to

hurt her feelings by saying "No" or, just as bad, "I don't know." We want to make her happy, but we don't want to get roped into something. The weaker, more-eager-to-please brothers among us might say yes before we're ready for that lifelong commitment. What happens then? We feel a growing sense of dread that we've made a mistake. We might even start resenting you.

If we were in no way intending to marry you but we were enjoying the relationship nonetheless, a rejected marriage proposal by the brother is going to instantly push the relationship onto bumpy ground. What are we supposed to do after that?

"Honey, I've been thinking. We've been doing this dating thing for almost two years now," she says, gazing sweetly into his eyes —which have instantly narrowed in suspicion.

"I think it's about time we took the next step," she continues, going on despite his obvious and growing discomfort. "Let's tie the knot. Let's get married. Okay?"

He tries to stay calm and not reveal his shock and anger at being put in this position. And he had really been enjoying his grilled salmon, too. Already she can tell by his response that she has made a bad move. She wants to say something else to ease the coming blow, but she holds herself back.

"Well, damn. That was unexpected," he says, wiping his brow with a napkin. He tries to smile, but it comes off looking like a pathetic grimace. He grows more angry at her for making him look pathetic.

"I, uh, well, I don't know. I'm not sure that I'm ready for that."

Are we expecting the sistah to forget the whole thing in this situation and ask the brother to pass the salt? Clearly, once she asks and gets an answer in the negative, there's a chance the whole relationship will blow apart into thousands of painful little shards—and no one within the explosion's radius will be spared the pain.

The safest thing for both parties is to talk about marriage enough before any proposal is dangled out there that you'd know with confidence what the answer is going to be. Spontaneity and whimsy are great for sex and romance, but in this arena they are usually as welcome as a toddler in a Tiffany store. The marriage proposal is a delicate creature.

We should consider the logistics of the thing, too. You ask, but I'm still supposed to go out and buy the ring? What if I don't have the requisite cash right now for a diamond ring purchase? What if I need a new transmission first, then I was planning on starting to save for a nice ring? If you propose, that takes all my planning and drop-kicks it into irrelevancy. I won't like that. But, hey, if you're doing the asking, maybe you're going to buy your own ring. That way, you can be sure of getting one you'd like. I wouldn't even need to be there with you for the shopping. You could bring a girlfriend. Then you could just cart it over to my place—certainly you'd need a wheelbarrow to carry it—to show me what you got. I'd nod and say, "That's nice, honey." Is that what you want?

Keeping It Alive

♥

Appearance After the Hookup: What's Wrong with Comfortable?

From a Sistah

Gravity is a bitch—and so is getting old. With each passing year, our bodies go the way of, like, an Olympic skier doing Mt. Everest—straight downhill. And our faces? Like an apple left in the fruit bowl just a tad too long. Y'all *know* what I'm talking about here. We check ourselves out in the mirror and there's another line circling under our eyes—and the smile we so proudly shined up in our man's face has some lines forming around it, too. We try to slip into those cute little linen trousers we wore proudly a few years back, and they can't get past the left thigh unless we grease it up with Crisco first. The hair? Seen less salt in a salt shaker. Oh, and 110 pounds? We ain't seen that side of slim in years.

Lena Horne gave me some good advice awhile back when I interviewed her for a story. The breathtakingly beautiful actress/

singer, then just days from her eightieth birthday and still very much a fly girl, told me that she doesn't preoccupy herself with trying to keep from growing old. "I think," she said, "you just have to look in the mirror and say, 'Look, this morning I got a few more wrinkles, and there ain't too much I can do about that.' "

Right.

That'd be easy enough if it was just you. But add a man with eyes into the equation, and it's pretty hard to ignore that your Coke-bottle figure, your perky breasts, your taut booty and your firm skin have been taken over by the invasion of the growing-old-and-can't-do-a-damn-thing-about-it body snatchers. They don't seem to take this getting old thing too easy. And who could blame them? Society makes women feel like we need to be sent to the animal shelter and put to sleep for getting old. Guys? They age, gain a little weight in the face, get a little gray around the edges, they're distinguished. Somehow, we got the message loud and clear that if a guy doesn't look the same exact way he did when we first met him, that's okay—because guys are supposed to age into this wise, handsome, debonair older gentleman. And that's despite the fact that he's put on extra extra pounds, his hair's fallen out and there're more wrinkles around his eyes and mouth than in the puss of a bulldog. We love him anyway.

Let that happen to a sistah.

Of course, it's the men who set this tone—this evil precedent that we women so readily accept as our fate. I've watched my mom grow older gracefully. She is more beautiful today than she was ten years ago, and ten years from now, she will be even more beautiful—even as more gray hair mixes with her auburn red, and her body settles into its older self. It's a function of nature—like the way a tree that was full of pink buds in the spring sheds its leaves for its winter slumber. People with a good eye see the beauty in both. So why is it that guys don't seem to get it?

Am I really that unbearable because I gained a coupla pounds and I don't look as young as I used to?

From a Brother

Okay, I'm about to commit one of the most heinous crimes ever witnessed in the sphere of male–female relations. I'm going to tell the truth about physical appearance: Men have an easier time loving women we find physically attractive.

Of course, I realize such a declaration puts me in danger of having my fingernails removed, one at a time, by a crazed gang of feminists. This isn't something that we do purposefully; we seem to have no choice in the matter. It is just the biological hand we have been dealt; not much different from the female cardinal or peacock casting an appreciative eye at the brilliant plumage of the parading males before making a mating decision. Perhaps it is our biological imperative at work, seeking the sleekest, strongest partner with whom to team up in producing superchild.

I'm not a psychologist—or a sociologist. My role here is not to do psychoanalysis of the male mind, or to dissect male socialization from infancy and theorize how that results in a male adult who so thoroughly prizes physical attractiveness that he'll approach the evillest, orneriest rattlesnake of a woman in the room if she's fine. I'll leave that to all the Ph.D.s whose books fill up the self-help sections of the mega-bookstore chains. (I hate to quarrel with one of those bestselling Ph.D.s, but I'm pretty damn sure I've never been to Mars.) I'm just trying to reveal a fundamental truth about men that women may find useful and that may explain many of our behaviors.

Women loudly proclaim that the male preoccupation with looks is superficial and causes us to overlook all those other wonderful qualities a woman may possess. We are chided for caring too much about what's on the outside. Sometimes I get tired of hearing that complaint, but I understand its sources and why it would bother the hell out of a woman. However, despite the complaints and the chiding, I don't think we're going to be able to change our stripes anytime soon.

In our early years, both boys and girls spend inordinate amounts of time obsessing over looks. Both sexes are drawn to the best-looking kids in the school; they acquire an air of importance and popularity that often seems related only to their physical appearance. What's clear is that there is some sort of biological imperative at work here—our young ones wouldn't be able to halt this behavior even if they desperately wanted to.

So we fast-forward ahead to adulthood, and we assume that adults will suddenly be able to shut down that internal meter that for years has honed itself into a finely tuned instrument to automatically rate another person's attractiveness? We now aren't supposed to care; it's no longer supposed to be deemed important because it's immature or politically incorrect?

Well, obviously we do care as adults. Men care AND women care. But women also learn to care about other things: financial stability, halitosis, the absence of a criminal record. Men care about these other things, too—but still not as much as looks. A woman could be as poor as a street beggar, with breath that could clear out a room and a rap sheet as long as our leg, but if she looks like Halle Berry we start thinking all we need is a container of Altoids, a visit to the women's section at Bloomingdale's and a perusal of the rap sheet to make sure her name didn't used to be Lorena Bobbitt. And we're good to go.

My opening statement should be read very carefully. I didn't say we would stop loving our mate if she put on a few pounds or started to look her age. But I do think it requires a little more mental energy for our love to stay as strong if we start thinking she's no longer physically attractive. That's not to say it's impossible. Just a little harder.

It's easier for the love to stay strong if we think our partner is still a jaw-dropping fly girl. That doesn't mean good looks is all we want in a wife—we're certainly capable of growing to despise a beautiful woman. But all other things being equal, I'd bet most men would stay around a little longer to try to "work things out" with the beauty than with the thickening dragon lady. When I was in college, if we wanted a quick check of an unseen woman's attractiveness, we'd ask the buddy who had seen her: Would you kick her out of bed if she farted? Crude, yes—but it does make the point.

Sometimes this can even affect how we feel about our partners on a day-to-day basis. When she's all dolled up and we're headed out to that New Year's Eve bash, we might find ourselves overwhelmed by our affection for our woman. Even if she tried, she'd probably be less likely to annoy us on this night than the week before when she threw on jeans and a sweatshirt to catch a late flick at the multiplex. Of course, we usually don't realize this is happening to us. Many men might even deny the words that I've just written. But I'm convinced that there's something larger going on here that is out of our control.

Does all this mean that men are bad people? Well, is a woman a bad person if she wants to marry a guy with a good income? So . . . why is there something wrong with us wanting something nice to look at for the rest of our lives? Does that make us evil? We're being unfair to ugly women, you say? We're not taking into account the effects of aging, you charge?

Okay, maybe you're right. But answer this: **Who would you choose to accompany you to your twenty-year high school reunion—a lazy, unemployed Denzel Washington or a lazy, unemployed Forest Whitaker?**

From a Sistah

Neither. We'd just as soon go alone. But we'd step into the room looking good—alone, but real good.

Okay, so, like, we sistahs don't mind getting dip. I mean, we can beat our faces with that Bobbi Brown blush and that Mac eye shadow and that Iman lipstick—lovely enough to make celebrity makeup artist Sam Fine envious. We can get those little Halle Berry cuts tight, those Brandy braids shining, those fly textured Afros and those naturals gleaming, step into that hottie dress and those fly Kenneth Cole strappy pumps and walk into the room fly girl down, like we own the joint. We sistahs clean up real nice. But Lord knows, there come some days when we don't feel like spit-shining everything before we leave the house. We might want to put that 'do in a ponytail, slip into those jeans and the skips with the not-so-clean shoestrings, the sweatshirt and the baseball cap, and roll around the corner to make a quick stop at the deli, or to the mall to pick up some essentials.

Fact of the matter is, sometimes we don't feel like getting all dolled up from head to toe 24–7–365. Let's face it; unless he truly is Sam Fine, most men don't understand what it takes to look good all day every day—and the implications behind it. We're women, and we've been told from the time we were baby girls that it was of the utmost importance for us to keep up appearances—to always smile, to always be pretty, to always look nice—because that's the only way society will have us. Anything less than that? Well, then you're not a woman, you're a slob, or you don't care about yourself, or, worst of all, you're a dyke bitch. Anything but a woman.

But we're not thinking about all of that when we slip into the down-day duds. We're simply trying to go on about our day comfortable—and, quite frankly, we don't find anything wrong with it. Shoot. Sometimes you just want to chill.

And sometimes you can't hold down that figure like you used to. Like, when we were in high school and college, if we walked to the end of the block, we lost 10 pounds. Working out wasn't necessary, but we did it every once in a while because it didn't seem, like, hard. Energy was in abundance, weight nonexistent. Then—boom! Gravity kicks in, the pounds get to gathering around the booty/thigh area, and basic maintenance becomes ridiculously hard. It's not that we don't want to look good; there's nothing we'd rather be able to do than to keep on looking like our twenty-two-year-old selves.

But we can't.

No matter how long we pedal that stationary bike—no matter how many memberships we get to Weight Watchers, Living Well Lady and Jenny Craig.

And you guys need to get over it.

This was true before we met you, this was true while we were getting with you, and it sure didn't change once we said, "I do." Sure, while we were dating you we dolled up a little bit more than usual, but you clean up when you're trying to make an impression. Who, after all, wants to scare away a potential good one by showing up to the date in a sweatsuit, all out of shape? It's obvious, though, that when we grow closer to the guy with whom we want to spend the rest of our lives, we'll be a little bit more comfortable being, well, comfortable around him. That's no disrespect or slight to him; we're simply dressing the way we did when he wasn't around us all day, every day. And just because we don't weigh the same amount we did when we met you, or our hair isn't as black as it used to be or gravity is kicking in, doesn't mean we're somehow not the same woman we were when we first met you. It means we're aging—something we *all* do. Granted, we can all stand to work a bit harder at keeping that young look about us—perhaps by taking up exercise, finding flattering styles for our graying pate, wearing clothes that make us every bit as sexy at age forty-five as we were at age thirty. But brothers would serve themselves well if they recognized that we're simply human.

Does the fact that we don't look like we did when you first met us mean that you're going to go off and find some young chippy to replace us?

From a Brother

Is that what you think, that our desire to have you look nice all the time is somehow a threat? Nah, babe, that's not it at all. We want you to look as nice as you can because we like when you look as nice as you can. If we give you any fever over the clothes you're wearing or the bulges you're growing, it's because we know you can do much better.

It's all about impressions. The less-than-kind might say ego. No matter how long a man has been married to or dating his woman, when he hits the street with her on his arm he wants the team to be as formidable as possible. He wants the brothers to look at his lady and shake their heads in admiration and envy. He wants the sistahs to look at his lady and say to themselves, "Damn, that brother must have it going on if he's stepping out with a lady who looks like that!" He wants the world to get the best possible impression of him, his abilities, his career status, his life choices. Because our women are a reflection of all those things. This society likes to think it can gain insights into people by the partners at their sides. We want people to think the best of us. At first blush, this may sound superficial, but I don't think it is. How much of our success at work and in life is dictated by people's impressions of us? After all, that's why we wear our most expensive outfits and linger extra-long on the tie or the shoes when we have an important engagement—we want others to get the best impression. So if we spend that much time picking out the damn tie, we certainly want our woman to look as tight and slammin' as possible.

Timing plays a major part here also. We get the most agitated when our ladies decide to go bummy on those occasions when we most care what people think. The problem is that our ladies don't always know when impressions matter most to us. As a service to you ladies, I offer the following guidance on the occasions when we care:

1. When we're going to a place where there will be many attractive black women.
2. When we're going to a place where there will be many important, rich, or well-known black men. (These first two places often coincide.)
3. When we're going to a place where we will see any of our co-workers.
4. When we're going to a place where we will see any males or females from our past, particularly our high school past or our college past.
5. When we're going to a place where there will likely be ex-girlfriends.
6. When we're going to a concert.
7. When we're going to a nightclub.
8. When we're going to a big-time professional sporting event.
9. When we're going to a fancy restaurant.
10. When we're going to a family reunion, or any event that surpasses the six-family-member threshold (weddings, funerals, baby showers, christenings . . .).

If ladies follow the guidelines in this list, they will magically avoid ever again seeing that scowl across their man's face as they walk out the door on their way to the car. And you must know that if we have gone to the next step of actually verbalizing our problem with your outfit, at the risk of putting any conversation or rhythm from you in a deep freeze maybe for the rest of the day, it means a great deal to us that you make some adjustments. 'Cause usually we'll do anything to avoid the deep freeze.

As for the fat, we understand that it's going to come. Lord knows we're grappling with the same monster ourselves in the belly area. But if it looks like you've thrown in the towel and given in to the monster, that's when we become concerned. That means eating all that fattening, greasy food every other day of the week without fitting any perspiration-inducing activities into the schedule. That means cookies and ice cream and bon-bons and videos without a treadmill, or exercise bike, or aerobics class, or early-morning power walk. That means no effort to halt the spread, to stave off the steady advance of cottage cheese across the body (booty). Sweets but no sweat.

If it takes you five minutes to catch your breath after one flight of stairs, and your sneakers' only purpose is to match that white short set, then I'm probably talking about you.

A bad attitude can also be a turnoff. The woman who has put on a few pounds but still sees herself as a fierce fly girl likely will still draw a twinkle in her man's eye. But the woman who beats herself up daily as she inhales the bon-bons will look even more like a lost cause to her man because she gives off those low self-esteem, I-hate-myself vibes.

Who's Responsible for My Happiness?

From a Sistah

Saw an episode of Oprah the other day, about some women who were victims of domestic violence who keep going back to their abusers. Oprah and a guest psychologist were getting all on those women— and rightfully so—about how they needed to just pack up their stuff and break north and never, ever return again, because those men weren't doing a damn thing for them but kickin' their behinds, putting their lives in danger, making them miserable and breaking their hearts. But through a sea of tears, each of the women kept defending their actions with one simple declaration: I need him because when he's not beating me, he makes me happy.

Of course, that set Oprah, the psychologist and the audience on fire, as the credo for the enlightened nineties woman was burning their tongues: You don't need a man to make you happy.

I can get with that, to some extent. Our generation is made up of that newfangled gal—the woman who can learn and earn and use both of those traits to stay self-sufficient. A man is her soulmate—her complement—not her necessity. She knows that it's nice to have a man, but she'd do just fine without him.

Thing is, though, that we want them. We talk about them, we think about them, we laugh about them, cry about them, pray for them, wish for them, hope someone finds one of them for us. And no matter how much we pretend we don't need him—no matter how many times *Iyanla,* Oprah and *Essence* drill it into our heads—we know that we do. You'd be hard-pressed to find a sistah who didn't, no matter how loudly she proclaims that she doesn't. This statement is not to be confused with that pathological need for a man, the need that would have us sistahs going through all sorts of changes and bending ourselves into all kinds of positions to accommodate him. There are a few sistahs who will contort themselves to make him happy and, in the process, lose themselves. But the majority of us, I think, are quite clear in that we know our lives would be that much better if we had a companion with whom to share all the good and bad times.

That's basically what this "gotta have a man" thing is all about. It's not about us being sad and when a man walks into our lives, we're all of a sudden happy again. We can be perfectly happy without him—but with him being there? Oooh—there's nothing like it.

And if he's going to be there, he might as well go on ahead and make us happy, right? I mean, we've gone all our lives expecting that we would have it all—that money would make us happy, that having a good career would make us happy, that having a family would make us happy, and that a man—especially a man—would make us happy.

And I don't think there's anything wrong with that, personally. When I was single, I had everything—a great career as a political reporter for the *Daily News,* (enough) money in the bank, a beautiful apartment in a great neighborhood in Brooklyn, good friends, a great nuclear family. And I was happy. I did the movies, I did plays, I went to parties, I went on trips with my girls. But there was many a night when I wished that I had a man. It wasn't just about wanting sex, it was about wanting male companionship. I wanted someone—a man other than my daddy—to hold me, to laugh with me, to make me feel safe in this world, to make me feel cherished, loved, happy. It wasn't about some kind of sick need to depend on a man; it was a healthy need for a mate—and there isn't an animal on this earth that doesn't search for one. Birds do it, bees do it, lions do it, monkeys do it, even mosquitoes do it.

Why can't women?

And why is it so unreasonable to expect that he will make me happy? We don't look for mates to make us angry, or sad, or melancholy, or mentally unhealthy. We look for him to make us happy. That means that he treats this relationship with the utmost respect, he brings his butt home at night, he contributes fully to raising our family, he helps around the house (without asking)—he does everything he's supposed to as a husband, father and lover. It's a mission—and when he's not on a mission to make us happy, then dammit, there's a problem and we will need it to be addressed quick, fast and in a hurry.

But for some reason, I gather, men think that they are not responsible for making us happy—that they have no obligation whatsoever to put smiles on our faces and make us feel good about ourselves and feel protected and loved. If we do feel those things, well, that's great. But if we don't, well, it must be our fault—because it certainly couldn't be his. It's a thinking that fully carries over into the larger society, which goes out of its way to tell us that we don't need men to make us happy—that we can be happy by ourselves. I beg to differ. To some extent, I think, we can. But it's all the more sweeter to have him on our arm. So how about it?

Who's responsible for our happiness?

From a Brother

This is one of the most important questions that any person in any relationship must answer. Counselors, therapists, psychiatrists, self help gurus and palm readers all make a bundle of loot trying to help people come to some measure of sanity with this question. Perhaps a more accurate wording for the question would be "How much responsibility should my partner carry in helping me find happiness?"

Things go wrong, we're all quick to look elsewhere in assigning blame. I'm just as guilty of this as anyone else. One of the hardest things is to admit when we're wrong. Especially to our mates, for some reason. Sometimes it feels easier to make this major admission at work, or on the playing field, or in the classroom, than it does at home with the person who means the most to us. It's almost as if we view our relationships at home like an ongoing war, and if we surrender any one battle it'll move us that much closer to losing the whole damn thing. Intellectually we know that it's supposed to be a partnership and that it works better if we act as though we believe it's a partnership, but we have a hard time keeping out the element of competition.

Well, if you fight too many battles at home, eventually you're not going to be able to see the mate as anything but an enemy. Any efforts at reconciliation will be met with mistrust. We'll feel the hostility and dread creep into our soul every time we pull up into the driveway; we'll quickly want to blame it on the enemy. And when you blame the enemy for whatever it is that ails you, you have handed over to someone else the power to control your own happiness, your own mental state.

Haven't you found that it is the people who seem to have the most confidence and are the happiest with themselves who can most easily admit that they're wrong? These are people who are totally in control of their own mental state; they would never think of giving someone else the power to drag them into the doldrums. You run into these warm, giving people and you daydream about how wonderful it must be to be married to that person—or to BE that person. You sense that they'd be able to admit to their mates or anyone else when they're wrong, then they'd smile and not think twice about it—because they're in *control*. They could confess that they had no idea what they were talking about, then reach out and envelop their partners in a big, luscious hug—because they're in *control*. That's a state I would love to one day say that I've achieved—to be able to admit I'm wrong to my love or anyone else, then spread my arms and wrap her inside. Once I'm able to do that, I'll know that I am in control and have assumed full responsibility for my happiness—and anything she adds to it is gravy.

Of course, most of us are as close to this ideal soul as we are to Mother Teresa. Instead, we have to struggle every day with those little demons that tell us that the person on the other side of the bed—the one who forgot to take out the trash, buy the groceries, pick up Latisha from soccer practice, make dinner, pay the paper boy, pay the phone bill—is the reason why we feel so tired, or lonely, or hungry, or horny, or poor. But when we manage to beat back the demons, we know that we have also let things slip our minds, or didn't have enough in the account to pay our share of the rent, or had to work late and couldn't play soccer mom, or had to take a business trip and leave our partner behind while his mother was sick. In other words, none of us are perfect, yet we act as if our past has been error-free when that special person in our lives messes up. I will try to devote myself to looking inward when I want to throw blame outward, hoping to one day get to the point where I can quickly forgive others for their transgressions because I'll know I've been there myself.

Of course, I'm not talking here about the extreme cases. If your man makes a habit out of treating your face and body like Rocky did that side of beef in the warehouse, then you're damn right to blame him for your temporary unhappiness. But what are you doing about your unhappiness in the long term? In other words, get the hell out of there. If your lady just can't seem to put down that crack pipe, no matter how hard homegirl tries, the world will understand if you decide that you're tired of your VCRs disappearing in the middle of the night.

In a woman's mind, what's the difference between a man being happy with himself and in love with himself—and how important are these traits?

From a Sistah

A man who is happy with himself is the best thing in the world, because he is confident and can handle his business. A brother who's in love with himself sucks.

There's nothing worse than a man who needs to be stroked—because we sistahs get pretty tired pretty fast of stroking. Don't get us wrong; we have no problem telling him he's beautiful. But none of that works when he's so busy elbowing us out of the mirror that he can't stroke back. Take, for instance, my girlfriend's (thank God he's an) ex-boyfriend. He was handsome as all get-out—just oozed sex. Had piercing dark brown almond-shaped eyes, and stark perfectly shaped eyebrows that always looked like they'd been painted on his face, and kissable, thick red lips and straight, pretty white teeth and a headful of black, curly locks. The boy dressed his behind off, too.

All of this, of course, carried well into the way he acted. He was a prima donna, a need-to-be-seen kinda person who had to be the prettiest in the room, who had to be the most talkative in the room, who had to be the smartest in the room—who had to constantly prove that he was The Man.

None of this would have been an issue if he indeed was The Man—but he wasn't. He wasn't all that smart, just loud and boisterous and more willing to make his stupid little points, no matter how wrong they might have been. He figured that if he just out-talked you, you'd eventually come around to his point—but the only reason you ended up agreeing with him was because you just wanted to shut him up. But he never realized it because he was The Man. And this particular man made a point of using his insecurities to make my girlfriend feel simply horrible about herself. He'd get into a debate with her on some remote subject like twentieth-century Tibetan politics, and then make her feel like she was the stupidest person on this earth because she didn't know the Dalaï Lama's philosophy on war. And then he'd test her—test her, y'all—on current events, make my girl feel like she had to memorize *The New York Times* daily in order to keep up with his expounding on world affairs. He'd also hold a special court sometime during the day to tell her about the way she dressed, or what she ate, or the way she combed her hair, and how she needed to change herself if she was going to be a better person.

He figured he was perfect, and he was trying to mold her into this perfect woman worthy of his love.

We all knew that homeboy was the furthest from perfect you could possibly get. Sure, he looked good, and he talked a good game, but anyone who needed to make my girlfriend, who happens to be a really sweet, beautiful, smart woman, into a total dimwit to make himself feel better about himself, was, well, an ass. A big, fat, nasty, hairy one.

He was in love with himself. In his quest to make himself feel and look better, he needed to belittle everyone surrounding him. The first victim of his charade was his woman.

We sistahs don't need men like that. We need brothers who are happy with themselves and happy with us—the way we are. We need him to compliment us and adore us and act like what we say matters—to agree with us without being disagreeable, to accept our faults and to love us anyway. We are ready, willing and able to do the same—but not for a man who is so enamored of himself that he disregards our needs and, worse, makes us feel guilty for having them. He is happy, and when he's happy, we're happy. When he's stuck on himself, I'll bet you any amount of money, honey, that he's got some problems that need to be addressed, and a strong, independent sistah who wants to be happy isn't going to be able to do anything for him but keep company in his stupid little pity party.

No thanks—we'll take the brother who's happy with himself—quirks, hangups, normality and all—any day of the week. He's the one who will truly keep us on our happy toes. In the meantime, answer us this:

Do brothers think sistahs depend too much on them for our happiness?

From a Brother

There's the understatement of life. We sometimes think that you depend exclusively on us to make you happy.

In the play *Having Our Say* about the Delany sisters, who both lived well past the age of one hundred, the sisters surmise that they've lived so long because they weren't married and instead had each other. In other words, they never placed themselves in the no-win situation of looking to a man to provide them with the things that bring happiness.

I think it's no coincidence that married men live longer than married women. Or that single women live longer than married women.

Unfortunately, too many of us become autopilot husbands after the marriage has chugged along for a certain number of years. We stop doing a lot of the little things that used to make our woman smile. We stop paying as much attention to her. But we expect her to continue paying just as much attention to us, and she usually does—at great cost to her self-worth and personal happiness. Taking care of us, for too many women, becomes their raison d'être, particularly after the kids are gone. We smile blissfully and think we have a marriage made in heaven; she broils from the inside out and worries herself to death.

A major benefit to women who depend on themselves for their happiness is their tendency to ask for what they want rather than expect us to read their minds. This brings us back to the old debate about whether a husband in sync with his partner's needs should be able to read her mind and anticipate her desires. I say, No, never. Many women say, Yes, of course. But a woman who is going out there and getting hers is going to lay it on the table for us. She's not waiting. She's taking responsibility. And we're all much better off because of it.

If I had to point to one thing that was consistent in most of my failed relationships, it was my partner's general unhappiness. Even if I ultimately was not the cause of her displeasure with her life, I'd be swept along in the whole tidal wave of blame. Whatever I was doing or failing to do that she didn't like became a reason to turn away from me. Usually it was termed "support"—i.e., I didn't provide her with enough "support."

When I hear that word it's going to break me out in hives for the rest of my life, 'cause there's nothing scarier to a man than getting smacked with the "unsupportive" label. It's so vague and unsettling, so internal and nebulous, that we feel as capable of correcting it as we do of easing your cramps. Does it mean we don't hug you enough? Or maybe we don't look up from the TV quick enough during the game when you ask us a question? We don't ask about your day soon enough when you enter the house? What is it? And is it always the same, or does it change every week? I suspect it changes. That means we're always chasing a sly, bruising, slick apparition. In your eyes, it's right there in front of us—but all we see is air. We try to reach out and grab it and come up with . . . nothing. You think we're stupid and clueless. And we are.

Arrgh! I better stop now—I'm starting to itch.

Sex: Hell Yeah It Still Matters

From a Sistah

You know, there just ain't a thing on this earth that can compare to making love with someone with whom you're falling in love. He's courted you, taken you to fine, romantic places—treated you like the lady you are. And in your mind, you imagine what it would be like to lay down with him—how sweet and sensitive he would be, how he would caress you from the top of your head to the bottom of your feet—just make your toes curl.

Love does that.

And that first night, when you know it's on, the butterflies gather up in your stomach, fluttering in sweet anticipation. The doorbell rings, and you're nervous but excited nonetheless—ready to see what's under that packaging, ready to explore, ready to please and be pleased. Just plain ready.

Um, um, um—love does that, chile.

And it stays that way, that newness keeps the lovin' fresh. Makes you want seconds and thirds and fourths—in one night. Gives you superpower strength—can have you doing things you never thought your body could possibly do. And you enjoy the hell out of doing it because, damn, you in love.

You feel the same way when he says *I love you* the first time, the same way when he says he wants you and only you, the same way when he pulls that box with that shiny diamond out of his breast pocket over a candlelit dinner, the same way when he walks you down that aisle. And the honeymoon? No bed of yours has ever seen that much action.

But then, get home, get back to work and the everyday hustle and bustle of life, get back into your social organizations, get back in good with your girlfriends and your mama and everyone else you ignored while you were getting it on with your man, and you sort of get comfortable. You get happy with the status quo—and all things personal get replaced by the quickie. The candlelight dinners by the fireplace you so lovingly prepared in the beginning of the relationship? Oh, who has time for that when you can just pop a few potatoes in the microwave for a quickie dinner? The long strolls around the park you used to take with him as the sun set every other evening? Um, the sun setting in the window next to your computer will have to do you.

And sex? Good grief. You don't have time to start with the massage, then go into the slow dancing, then head for the bubble bath and then to the sheets on the regular like you used to. Too much stuff to do in so little time. Something's got to take the back seat—and when you're tired, sex is the first thing to go.

This, of course, is particularly true when the partner is someone who's in your face 24–7–365. You figure, Shoot—he's here. He's not going anywhere. Do I really need to have sex with him every night? If I don't do it tonight, won't he be there, in the same position, on the same side of the bed, slobbing up the same pillow, snoring in the same rhythms, tomorrow night and the next night and the night after that, too?

So we get comfortable. We put off until tomorrow (or the day after that—or hell, next week) what you all would like to do tonight. And we get dogged out for it—get the back tossed to us, silent treatment and that heavy breath-sighing if we say, "Not tonight, honey"—as if our saying "no" tonight means "no—not ever." **What's up with that? Does sex really matter as much after the marriage or later in the relationship as it did early on?**

From a Brother

*Is the sky blue? Is Johnnie Cochran smooth? Is Mike Tyson still the scariest brother on the planet? Hell, yeah. I would say that sex later in the relationship or marriage is **more** important than sex early on if the coupling is going to have any staying power.*

Put simplistically, a couple with a happy, healthy sex life is likely to be a happy, healthy couple. That doesn't mean that sex is the most important thing in a relationship or a marriage, but if it's not happening you can bet your bottom dollar (my apologies to Don Cornelius) that something is wrong and the thing is eventually going to crash and burn. The lack of moaning and groaning is a symptom of a dysfunctional relationship—it doesn't cause it, just as much more is required to keep the thing strong besides a lot of boning.

I think most couples know this instinctively, but that doesn't make the logistics any easier. At first it seemed that when we got together, sex was usually the ultimate destination. Both parties expected it, planned for it, looked forward to it. So tiredness, sleepiness, headaches, television, phone calls—all those things that can frequently cause *coitus ain'thappeningus*—are pushed aside in pursuit of the swerve. This is understood by both parties; no further planning or discussion is needed. So we never get in the habit of talking about when we're going to do it. When we get together, we just do it.

Once we slide the rings on the fingers or get into a routine in the relationship, things start changing. We're in the house together every single night. On some of those nights we're not going to have sex. Brothers understand that. We don't have a problem with that—well, most of us could do it almost every night if given the chance, but we know that's not likely. But how do we know on which nights you do want to have sex? 'Cause that's what this often comes down to—how does our mate let us know when she's horny? Sometimes the sistah will make things easy by tossing her panties over our head, or flashing some booty as she heads toward the bedroom. But that's not going to happen every time. Not even most of the time. Sometimes she might be open to sex, but she's going to need just a little nudge. How can we identify one of these particular nights? Well, we can't. And that's a problem.

When we enter adulthood, we become a little more comfortable talking about sex. In those early years we made our move and hoped for the best. But when we get hitched in marriage or a serious relationship, we don't always want to have to make the move and possibly get dissed. It still hurts to get dissed, even if it's your loving wifey doing the dissing. We will still try to avoid this quick flash of pain. That means we're not going to be eager to ask for sex, because you might say "No." That means there will be some nights when we'll lie there and wonder if we could have gotten some if only we had tried a little harder. And there will be other nights when we will lie there silently stewing in our juices because we asked and got turned down.

All these difficulties make relationship sex more complicated than we ever thought it would be when we dreamed about having a beautiful woman laying next to us every night. Compound the problem when children enter the picture and career pressures start sucking the sexuality right out of us and you soon have a marriage with an unhealthy, dysfunctional sexual relationship.

It would make things a lot easier on us if we could work out some kind of system with our mates. We'd need a signal of sorts to let us know if we were going to get lucky that night. This would relieve us from the pressure of trying to guess and rescue us from the possibility that you will summarily reject our entreaty. A pair of panties left on the bathroom doorknob, or a bra on the lampshade, or—my personal favorite—the absence of a t-shirt or nightgown or any other article of sleepwear when you crawl into the bed would work as clear-cut billboards announcing your desires. Of course, for the bolder females out there, simply announcing to your man that you want to get busy tonight will work just fine.

What happens when the sex life in a serious relationship or marriage starts turning sour? You know what happens: the man starts looking elsewhere. Just because his wife is no longer willing or interested doesn't cause a man's sex drive to shut down. This sounds like common sense to me, but many women act as if this bit of sense has never penetrated their cerebrums. They get upset at their men and decide to use sex as a weapon: They deny him the sweet stuff, figuring he'll learn his lesson. But this is no kind of solution. Whatever the problem was won't get solved, and the man will start thinking his woman is giving him a tacit license to go out there and find it somewhere else. Once that happens, they've started down that slippery slope and it's real hard to climb back up.

So, to make things easier on your mates, could you give us a signal or a yell or something when you want to do it?

From a Sistah

We don't mind tossing you a little bare booty every now and then to let you know we're down, but if you're going to wait for a signal from us every time you're ready to get your swerve on, you're probably going to go to bed disappointed a lot.

We sistahs are not in the business of doing a certain number of things: We don't initiate the first dance, we don't offer to buy the first drink, we definitely don't ask for your hand in marriage—and to be so incredibly aggressive as to be in charge of setting *it* off? Oh, prepare to be frustrated like a mug, buddy.

Not to say that any of that is right. I've always said that we sistahs—the nineties ones, at least—need to let go of that frame of reference that dictates we act a bit shy and aloof when we're dealing with our men. There's just no need for that today. We are strong and bold and proud and intelligent and we have careers and we pay bills and we make decisions about our lives. But as soon as it comes to dealing with our men, we lose it—revert right back to Ozzie-and-Harriet mode. We yield to the man in almost every way, giving him free range to make the decisions on everything from where we're going tonight to which region of the country we're going to live in. And without a shadow of a doubt, that thinking filters right on down to all matters of the heart.

That means that we're not going to be the ones to make the moves on or with brothers—particularly the ones in the boudoir.

Yes, yes, we love making love—have no problems with getting our worlds rocked. But we'd much rather you initiate it, rather than be forced to tell you when we want to get it on. For some of us sistahs, taking that kind of initiative when we were dating was considered fast, and I think that carries over into the long-term relationship—just a bit less pronounced. Weird, but true.

Perhaps even more of a reason why we're not going to toss you that signal as much as you'd like is because we just don't want to have sex as much as you guys do. We get the feeling that if presented with the opportunity, you all would want to knock boots twice a day, every day. We wouldn't—and we won't, ever. The fact of the matter is—and I'm disclosing some stuff here that perhaps I shouldn't, but since we're coming clean, I might as well let you know—we committed sistahs aren't exactly into having sex on a consistent basis. We're preoccupied with work, the kids, Mom's illness, Daddy's bills, our bills, more work. And all of that tends to get us a bit, well, distracted. At the end of a long, hard day at the office and a long, hard day on the homefront—sorry, we're not thinking about getting it on. We're thinking about sleep—preparing our bodies and our minds for the next day. We're trying desperately to rid ourselves of all the anxieties and fears we faced during the day, and we're just plain exhausted by all the mess we put up with. Having sex at the end of all that can be, well, a bit of a chore, at least—a pain in the ass if we're especially bothered.

That doesn't mean we're cold fish, or that we're not sexual. We are. Nothing turns us on more than our beautiful men. We're just not on the same energetic wave as you brothers when we get older and into a more stable relationship. If we do it tonight, that's great—it's wonderful. But if we don't do it tonight, our earth is not going to crumble. We'll just get—and happily accept, thank you—more sleep. And it will be like that most nights if you don't set it off, because chances are we're not going to do it, unless, of course, we are feeling especially frisky.

That means that it's on you, dear, to make the moves. If you want it, come get it. Nothing too pushy, nothing too over the top. We DO NOT want you attacking us, or forcing the issue, or being ridiculously insistent. And we definitely don't want you to make us feel guilty for not being in the mood—for wanting to cuddle the pillow instead of you. The bottom line is, if you want it more often, you better ask for it—and you damn well better understand the signals for when we're just not in the mood. And it would help if you respected that.

You all would be wise to learn how to get us in the mood a little bit better, too. There's nothing more annoying—or less sexually stimulating—than being fêted by your man the same exact way every night. You know the deal: Get up, go to work, come home, have dinner, watch a little TV, brush your teeth, pull out your clothes for work tomorrow, get in the bed, get a snuggle from him and a tap from somewhere else on him, and the next thing you know, you're having sex—for a few minutes. Then somebody—I'm not going to call out any sexes or point any fingers or anything—rolls over and goes to sleep.

Then, like clockwork, two days later—the same deal.

Uh, boring.

How's about a little excitement—before the climax? How's about a little tenderness, a little romance—something more than the fifteen-minute special? Just think about it: We'd enjoy it a bit more this time, and the next time around, we'd remember what we got the last time around and, whammo! You're in there.

But that's hard work. We know that you don't want to put on a full-scale romantic seduction episode every time we get to doin' the do. With today's fast pace, nobody has time to brush his teeth, set out his suit and socks *and* set the scene for a romantic interlude before we settle in for the night. But dang—can you work with us on this one? Maybe just a little bit?

And if we're not in the mood, accept the fact that we're not in the mood. We're not going anywhere—we'll be here tomorrow and the next day and the day after that. Recognize that the last time we had sex was not the last time we're going to have sex— if there's nothing wrong with the relationship, of course. Our telling you that we're not in the mood is just that: We're not in the mood. It doesn't mean we're less sexually attracted to you, that we don't want you to touch us, ever. It means we just don't want you to touch us in that way tonight.

Of course, this doesn't seem to go over too well with the brothers. So perhaps you could answer this: **Why do you all take** it so personal if we don't want to have sex whenever you guys want to have sex?

From a Brother

Because we never get used to getting dissed, that's why. We're still thinking of the women who wouldn't dance with us in the night-clubs, the cheerleaders who wouldn't smile at us in the hall, the nasty girl down the block who played doctor with every snot-nosed kid except us, the pretty girls who took our business cards but never called, the ugly girl who took our business card and had the nerve not to call . . . You get the point.

Just because you're our mate doesn't mean that hearing "No" becomes any easier. In fact, some of us thought we would be freed of ever being rudely rejected once we slid the ring on that left hand—only to find out we couldn't have been more stupidly wrong.

To make things harder on us, our mates sometimes send out mixed signals. A sexy commercial comes on television, she looks at us suggestively and makes some vague comment about what's gonna happen "later." Immediately we're titillated and horny and become a walking, talking erection for the next two hours, waiting. We figure once she's finished watching TV and brushing her teeth and flossing and washing her face with all that goo and putting up her hair and thinking about what she's wearing the next day . . . then she's gonna give us some. But once she's done all her various pre-bedtime chores, she crawls beneath the sheets, we smoothly turn her way, smiling like a kid in a big-ass candy store, and we get, "Oh, babe, I'm just too sleepy." We're shocked, floored, devastated. We KNEW we were gonna get some. What about the commercial? Tired? Shoot, we can count on one hand the times we've been too tired to get some. We're NEVER too tired. So we don't understand too tired. Especially when you virtually promised it was going to happen. Tired? Damn, you must have been messing with us, 'cause you didn't look tired when you were washing your face for a half-hour.

These are the kinds of thoughts that go through our minds when we get rejected. It's a dis, no matter how much you try to sugarcoat it and say it's not "personal." Hell yeah it's personal—it wasn't directed at the guy down the hall or the fat dude across the street. *We* were told "No." That's a dis, and we don't like disses. We've never liked disses, and just because we're married or in a serious relationship doesn't make them any easier to take.

Family Affairs: Mama, Daddy and Us

From a Sistah

It's true what they say about getting hitched: It is absolutely one of the happiest days in a girl's life—and I'm no exception to that rule. Our wedding was truly spectacular: a simple, elegant, African-inspired affair in a beautiful museum in Soho, New York City. Surrounded by about seventy-five of our loved ones, Nick and I looked into each other's eyes and vowed before God to love, protect and respect one another. We even promised that if the other made us mad, we would forgive—because we're in this "until death do us part." After we said our vows, we poured libations and we did something that was extremely important to both of us: We created a family unity ritual—one in which our parents gave our nuptials their blessing.

That final piece was, perhaps, just as important as the vows and the calling of the ancestors, as we are both extremely close to our parents. We've learned from them and loved them all our lives, emulated them in a lot of ways and continuously ask the creator to bless us with their wisdom and strength. We both recognize every day of the year, every minute of the day, that we are blessed.

Let me tell you this much, though: Had my daddy not liked this man, there would have been problems. Serious problems. See, my dad is, next to my husband, my very best friend. We've always been tight—always giggled together, always talked about anything under the sun, always got into trouble with Mom or simply drove her crazy with our silliness. When I was little, we'd go to the mall and get big ol' ice cream cones and sit on the benches and just sit and people-watch—make fun of the funny-looking folks—or we'd simply get in the car, me riding shotgun, and make the rounds to the dry cleaners and Penney's and Sears and Macy's so he could pay the bills before we went somewhere neat like Burger King or something. To this day, we still get together to watch the fights (we almost always put our money on the same guy), and you'd be hard-pressed to find a Knicks game we haven't analyzed together.

Simply put, my daddy is my boy—the first man I've ever loved. And while I haven't always followed his advice to the tee, I have always taken it into account—particularly when it came to my men.

Same thing goes for Bettye Boop, my mom—who has an uncanny ability to read Negroes the moment they darken her doorway. She knows how to pick 'em—my daddy should be clear evidence of that. She's a wise woman, a pretty lady with impeccable taste who taught me how to love God and not take any mess.

With those two in my corner, it was really easy to know what was good for me—to understand what true love is. And we are thisclose. So it only made sense that I marry someone who would understand it, accept it and want to be a part of my family.

Now, someone who doesn't know me or my family might be inclined to think that my 'rents run my life, that a brother wouldn't have a chance against those two. It would be easy for him to assume that I don't have a mind of my own, that I'm too dependent on Bettye and Jimmy for my peace of mind. And he might run in the complete opposite direction once he saw how tight we three are. Thank God Nick comes from a close-knit family and could understand the relationship I share with my parents.

Other sistahs aren't as fortunate, though, because some brothers tend to trip when Mommy and/or Daddy or any other immediate family member is around. Accusations will free-fall, with him accusing her of picking family over him, of respecting their opinions over his and all kinds of other things that turn family ties into a relationship liability, rather than the asset that they should be. This, of course, presents a problem, as we can't expect to cut off fam for some dude—but at the same time, we don't want to tell brotherman just to step.

Do men think getting in good with the family is as important as women think it is?

From a Brother

We feel the same flutter of nervousness as you sistahs do when we're about to go before that particular jury. If we're really into the sistah—and we wouldn't have let her talk us into a visit to the folks if we weren't—we know there's no first impression as important as the one you make when that front door first swings open.

Just as enduring a symbol in our community as the mother putting a potential daughter-in-law through the paces is the daddy giving a possible son-in-law the third degree as he determines whether the boy is good enough for his little girl. Even if her mom and dad are warm and easygoing, we know our chances of escorting little Latoya down the aisle will be severely hampered if we don't take out the gold tooth cap and the nose ring.

Although many women climb through the professional ranks these days for years—often in cities far from mom and dad—before they even start thinking about marriage, it doesn't mean that the parents don't still hold a great deal of influence in the decisionmaking process. We're not dumb; we know this big-time. That's why we're going to try to hold off the visit to the homestead for as long as possible.

Sometimes the home visit can be tricky because there may be an unpleasant sister or an aunt who holds much sway over our lovely lady's view of the world. We spend precious hours kissing up to Mom, desperately trying to remember which fork to use, covering our mouths when we yawn, even refraining from talking with our mouths full, only to find out the next day that our lobbying was misdirected—the real seat of power and influence resided in the expansive seat of Aunt Sharon, who sat over in the corner frowning at us for three hours and sucking her teeth whenever we tried to engage her in conversation. With the Aunt Sharons of the world, it's often factors beyond your control that put you on her booty list—your skin is too dark, your skin is too light, your family doesn't have enough money, your family has too much money and thinks they're better than somebody, your nose is too big, you're too short, your clothes are too tacky, you got on too much jewelry (okay, these last two are within your control, but you had asked your girl when you were getting dressed whether the outfit would pass muster with Mom, NOT Aunt Sharon).

What I have found is that if we try real hard and make the future in-laws into allies, it can be helpful in our love relationship. When our lady is acting up or acting out, only Mom and Dad can put a voice to what we are thinking but might not say: Homegirl is being a spoiled brat. In resolving disputes, the parents might even be eager to take our side if they really like us because they know it'll do more long-term damage if they take the side of their little girl and risk making the hubby/boyfriend into an enemy of the whole family.

I wonder about this one, though: If my woman is extremely close to her mother or father or both parents, is it up to me or up to her to make me more a part of her family? In other words, if I'm going to be spending time around my new woman and her family, how do I avoid feeling left out?

From a Sistah

It's the responsibility of both parties, but you brothers damn sure better get used to puckering up if you truly want to get in good with the folks.

Chances are that if the sistah likes you a whole lot, she's going to do everything within her power to get you and her parents to get along. She wants the people she loves the most to fall in love with you so that your union with her will be comfortable—seeing as relationships are already hard enough to deal with without your mama and daddy telling you that your man ain't worth the fertilizer she sprinkled on her azaleas. So she's going to show you off like a four-year-old does a shiny new quarter, and she is going to set you all up in situations where you will have no choice but to speak and socialize with one another. If she wasn't truly interested in you, she wouldn't bother.

But she can only do so much.

If you've been invited to the coveted Thanksgiving table, and her mom threw down on a "soul food" type feast, sat you down at the table, put a napkin in your lap and tried her best to engage you in some conversation, and all you can do is grunt, burp and give her one-word answers to her grilling—er, questions—then there will be absolutely nothing your lady will be able to do to save face for you. You've dug your hole, and you'd be best to crawl right into it, because her mom is going to talk about you good before the doorknob hits ya where the good Lord split ya for that kind of behavior.

I had a boyfriend once who got invited to a holiday dinner. He showed up just in time to eat, which would have been okay if homeboy would have lookcd up from his plate every once in a while and participated in some grown-folk talk. My mom just took it as him being hungry and nervous, and dismissed it. But after dessert, when everyone just sort of lounged around in the dining room area sipping soda and rubbing their stomachs and just kickin' it, this Negro had the nerve to go sit on the couch, pull out a book, and proceed to read to himself while everyone else was talking. Every once in a while, he would look up and say something—but it was only to disagree with snatches of the conversation and offer his own high-horse opinion.

My mother didn't even wait for homeboy to leave; she just talked about him like a dog—and hoped he could hear it, too, because Mom can be kinda raw like that. Our relationship was doomed from there; I just couldn't imagine being with a guy who didn't have courtesy or respect for his elders, let alone my parents.

You don't want to put yourself in that kind of situation. If you've been invited to your girl's parents' crib, be polite, be courteous, participate in the conversation, don't be judgmental and definitely, without a shadow of a doubt, suck up. Don't go overboard with it; nobody likes a syrupy asskisser.

Lollipop-sweet cheek pincher is good.

Now how about your mama? If she doesn't like me, does that mean I'm going to automatically get the boot?

From a Brother

No, you won't automatically get the boot, but if she doesn't like you it will probably put into motion a dozen little whirring engines that eventually will start wearing away at the relationship. Think of it as the slow-motion boot.

Yes, we care what our mamas think. I don't think there's anything wrong with that, as long as we don't take it too far. Relationships with females can end; our relationship with our mother never ends. She's going to be the one consistent woman in our lives for the rest of our lives, even when she remains in spirit only. With my mother, Migozo, her lessons stay with me always, her voice a whisper or a shout in the back of my head, even if she's a thousand miles away. She's always there, like an enveloping presence, a voice of reason or doubt, in Surround Sound. It's pretty hard for any woman to compete with all that. And if she doesn't like you, that's what it's going to become, a competition—with my sorry behind caught in the middle.

From experience, I can tell you the dynamic is this: The mother vibes start kicking in, telling Mom that this woman isn't going to work. The woman starts picking up these bad mother-vibes. Or perhaps the woman gives off bad vibes around the mother that Mom starts to pick up on. Whichever way it happens, the result is that they don't much enjoy being around each other. Seeing all this transpiring in front of him and feeling quite overwhelmed and powerless, the son does what most would in this situation—he tries to keep his mom and his woman apart. That might work wonderfully for his woman, but to Mom what it starts looking like is that this evil witch of a woman is keeping her son away from her. Once that happens, it's on. We might as well bring in ring announcer Michael Buffer to introduce the two prizefighters, 'cause it's gonna get ugly. Mom may not come right out and announce to her son that he needs to kick homegirl to the curb with a combat boot, but she will take every opportunity to let him know that perhaps his woman did this wrong, or she should be doing that instead. If and when problems crop up—and every relationship has problems—if he makes the mistake of sharing with Mom she'll insert the dagger and twist it around, adding another wound to the already laboring beast that is their love affair. Eventually, this wounded beast is going to collapse in a big heap. Mom will be standing over to the side, smiling.

I think what moms like to see is effort. They can even be reasonable in their expectations for their boy. Maybe instead of Halle Berry looks and Toni Morrison talent, she could have Toni Morrison looks and Halle Berry talent. But Halle Morrison must demonstrate that she cares about pleasing Mom. She doesn't have to kiss her entire behind all the time—just part of the behind part of the time. If she turns her back on this whole tradition of kissing Mom's booty, this centuries-old game, Mom will rightly think that homegirl has some attitude problems that need to be addressed. Mom will think these problems should get addressed elsewhere, with somebody else's son as the victim.

I must say that there may be some brothers out there whose mommies will call him up in his car phone as soon as he leaves the house and tell him to stop and deposit homegirl at the next intersection—and he'll dutifully stop the car and tell her she must get out because his momma said. These brothers have never learned to stand up to their mothers, and Mother isn't shy about taking advantage. If any of you sistahs are starting to suspect you might be sharing space with one of these brothers, you have several options:

- Run away.
- Walk away.
- Hire a hit man and have Mommy rubbed out.

Though the third option may sound as if it has the most long-range benefits, remember you'll have this torture to face: finding an outfit to wear to the funeral.

Work: Are We in Competition?

From a Sistah

We've been married for a few years, managed to put our little bit of money together to buy the things that married couples buy—a car, a house, nice things to put in said house. You've climbed the ladder at work, and I make a cute little penny, too. With our salaries combined, we're not hurting. Could always use more, but we're fine—we're comfortable, happy.

Then I come home with some great news: "Baby, I got a raise—can you believe it?"

You tell me that's great, and you're smiling from ear to ear until I mention that my boss's show of gratitude has managed to lurch my salary about $15,000 higher than yours. Suddenly, I can't see your teeth or the white of your eyes. Suddenly, there is silence. Suddenly, we're not as happy as we were when I came in with the great news.

A scenario, yes—but definitely not unrealistic. How many brothers on this here planet would take well the news that, after years of stability with him as the top money-earner in the house, his lady is now the one who's bringing home a larger share of the loot? I propose that it would be a huge problem—one that would cause a serious rift in a strong relationship. It just doesn't seem that brothers would be able to get over the insecurity they'd suffer knowing that she's more paid than them.

Of course, it doesn't work that way for us. Our man comes in the house talking about, "Honey—I got a raise," we're ready to celebrate. Where's the champagne? Let's go to dinner! What can we buy with this newfound money? We are happy because it means that we—not you, but we—have that much more to put in the bank. Even more importantly, we're ecstatic that our baby is getting some respect at the job.

But no, you can't be happy for us—can't say, "Congratulations, babes—where we going to celebrate?" I'd venture to say that we'd get mope faces and long mouths—and I'd bet that they'd be steeped in insecurity, that twirling around in the back of your mind would be the assumption that we're going to think we're better than you because we make more money than you. Am I right? **Would a brother feel insecure in our relationship if a sistah began making more money than him?**

From a Brother

This one is all about power and dominance in the household—issues that most couples want to avoid like the IRS. Most men enjoy the hell out of watching their woman climb the career ladder and seeing the family bank account grow. This is a good thing, not a bad thing. What we're afraid of is that as her bank account grows, there is a shift in the balance of power. So I would say that "insecure" isn't the right word to describe our feelings. "Apprehensive" might be better.

Most couples aren't comfortable talking about the balance of power in their relationships because it means one partner may be forced to confront the reality that their mate is more dominant than they are. Nobody, man or woman, wants to make an admission like that. But if cornered, most people, I bet, would acknowledge that many of their household arguments and conflicts occur when one partner tries to step out of their usual role and exert more decisionmaking authority or control than they are supposed to.

In a study of power on college campuses in the 1980s, sociologist Jacqueline Fleming found that African-American women enjoyed much more prestigious, impressive positions on predominantly white campuses—where they usually outnumbered African-American men—than they did on predominantly black campuses, where black men tended to take these positions. What this meant was that black women were able to flourish when there were fewer black men around to subjugate them.

In our households, the logical extension of this phenomenon would have black men trying to be dominant over their mates in decisionmaking authority. This is probably the expectation that many brothers have when they enter into a long-term relationship—that they will be able to get their women to do what they say. Some likely turn the expectation into a reality; many others probably find that things are much more complicated than that—in other words, if one spouse forces the other into decisions, eventually the weaker spouse is going to rebel and the whole thing will come crashing down. There usually needs to be something closer to a democracy for the relationship to work.

Black men fear that when the woman's salary starts to dwarf their own, the woman will look to take a dominant position. It may never happen, but he's going to constantly be on the lookout for the slightest change in tone or attitude to indicate that she believes she's in charge now because her pockets are fatter. Of course, women could have these same fears if their husbands start making a lot more money than they do. It certainly can cut both ways.

I think men AND women need to be aware of these sorts of fears if they find their salary starting to substantially outpace their mate's. Love relationships are a delicate balance; if one side begins to get outsized notions of his or her power, the whole balance will be destroyed. It would be ideal if the man or the woman could share their growing sense of unease over the shift in power if they see it coming—for instance, the brother could tell his sistah that he'd like for her to be sensitive of his feelings when they're trying to decide on their next car purchase. But I know such conversations are a whole lot to ask of any couple—they lay bare all kinds of feelings that most of us would rather take to our graves. In Amy Tan's *The Joy Luck Club*, the husband of one of the Chinese women she profiled insisted on all the household expenses being split fifty–fifty, even though she made only a fraction of his salary. This bothered the hell out of her, but she kept it all bottled up until it was too late.

Also, we have been conditioned to think that we're supposed to pay for stuff. Women play into this: Many women in a marriage or longtime relationship won't think twice about leaving the house without a dime in their pockets, secure in the knowledge that brotherman is going to pick up any checks that are thrown their way while they're out. The unspoken assumption here is that the man is supposed to have money in his pocket while his woman doesn't necessarily need to. But when she starts making a lot more money, more and more she's going to start suggesting that she pick up the tab. It's common sense. But many men still will be bothered when they see it happening. They may see it as a harbinger of her growing sense of dominance, or at least her feeling that she's more capable of paying than he is—which, of course, she is. These male feelings may be unfounded and unfortunate, but that doesn't stop them from coming.

When my wife's first book, *The Sistahs' Rules,* started flying off the shelves and she appeared on the couch next to Sinbad on *Vibe,* and on BET, CNN and many other shows, I started getting kidded by friends who jokingly referring to me as "Steadman" in reference to Oprah's longtime beau. Their point was that I was beginning to get overshadowed by my woman. This seemed to tickle people, men and women. At first, I'll admit, it bothered me a bit, particularly since we're in the same profession, but I would have been appalled with myself if I ever let it become an actual issue that I forced her to deal with. That would have been punishing her for her success. I realized it was my ego that was causing me discomfort; it would have been incredibly lame on my part to let my own insecurities feed on themselves and grow to the point where they became "problems" between us. That I refused to do.

What would be easiest in answering the question of who pays is if both parties dump much of their disposable income into one huge pot, so then it doesn't matter whose hand is dipping into the pot to pay the check because both of them contributed to it. This income sharing may be harder for some people than others, but it may work to shield hurt feelings if the couple can pull it off.

Don't women also have an expectation that the man is supposed to make more money—and don't many women secretly enjoy little jokes at the man's expense if his wife brings home significantly more bread—i.e., Steadman and Oprah, Roseanne and Tom Arnold, Whitney and Bobby, Madonna and whoever she happens to be with this week?

From a Sistah

Yes, we expect you to make more money, but we're not going to think any less of you if you don't—and no, we don't get off on the "Steadman" jokes, because the last thing we want to do is have our men walking around all insecure with our success and taking it out on us.

Let's set the record straight: We do want you to make more money because that's what we've been taught to expect—and it makes all the sense in the world to us to do so. Just think about it: When we marry and agree to start a family, one of us is going to have to leave work and have the baby, and the other one is going to have to keep working to financially support our family. Now, we can't wait until some scientist—and no doubt she will be a woman—figures out how to arrange it so that men can bear some kids. But until that time comes, we sistahs are the ones who have to birth the babies and stay home with them for the first months—sometimes even years—of their lives. And when we do, who's going to take care of us? We already know that the family leave laws are overly oppressive; who can afford these days to take six months' unpaid leave to bond with a newborn? No paycheck from us means that our man's paycheck will have to suffice. We'd be much more secure in the fact that he'd have the money for those diapers and that formula if he made more than we did.

It's just simple mathematics.

Some of us do tend, however, to get caught up in that old-fashioned notion that our men are supposed to be more wealthy than us, just because. But you can assign that blame to society in general, and your own lot, particularly, because it is you all who take special care to maintain power in the workplace by awarding yourselves the higher positions and salaries. You're absolutely right when you argue that it's a matter of the balance of power—and you all have done a pretty good job of making sure you're on top, that it is you and only you who wields that power, and that we're either playing runner-up or standing on the sidelines watching (and, in some cases, quite happy to do so).

Those notions seep right into the household, where you all have been so incredibly used to making decisions on all matters pertaining to the purse that you've been reluctant to give up the strings. And we're often in no position to grab them from you—or want to, for that matter, for fear that we'll lose you over something so completely stupid as an argument over who makes more money and therefore should make the money decisions. In a perfect world, we would make those decisions together—but how comfortable are you brothers with that? Suffice to say, most sistahs probably think you'd be more comfortable in RuPaul's high heels and lipstick than you would with that one.

So we play along to get along—either find us a man who is paid more than we, or turn ourselves inside out to make sure that he doesn't get the impression that we think we're better than him when it comes to the finances. It is no easy task, particularly when the outside world is watching. Nothing made me wince more than when people took it upon themselves to tease my husband by calling him my "Steadman." Shoot: I'm sure Oprah doesn't appreciate anyone ranking on her man, either, and pretending that she is dating a "kept man." I know that my husband works hard, that he contributes a nice amount of money to our household, and that he has more talent in his pinky toe than most people dream of having. It's part of the reason why I married him. He didn't all of a sudden become a trifling, dependent, lazy degenerate the moment I got a book deal. I'm sure that the same holds true for Steadman, who was a smart businessman in his own right when he decided to take up with a then-not-so-rich Oprah, before she got famous. I'm sure that like me, she is bothered by the inference that she'd be smart enough to become one of the richest and well-regarded women in the world, but too dumb to realize that a man is ganking her bank.

Please. Give us some credit. An insult to our man is an insult to us.

Is it ever possible for a sistah to assert herself on issues concerning money without her man thinking she is wielding the power in the relationship?

From a Brother

Sure it's possible. But the devil is in the details. It's all a matter of **how** *she does it.*

As with most things, there's a right way and a wrong way. The wrong way would be for the sistah, intent on "asserting herself," to charge right to the heart of the matter and tell him they're painting their bedroom pink because she pays the bulk of the mortgage and if she wants a pink bedroom, dammit, she's gonna have a pink bedroom—even if it makes him feel like the weakest panty lace on the block. This may not be what you intended by the word "assert," but it's the kind of image that comes to mind. "Assert" is a scary word. It conjures up visions of a neck-rolling, finger-waving, left-hand-on-hip sistah in full outrage mode ordering some man to bend to her will because she's more important at work, in the family and in the relationship. Even if she doesn't come right out and say she pays more of the mortgage, she'll set him off anyway if he thinks she's trying to pull a power play.

Making decisions is a tricky thing for any two people who are supposed to be partners—whether it's in a dry-cleaning business or a marriage. It is often during those tense times when we have to make the toughest decisions that we do or say the stupidest things that we come to regret. Should we use the vacation money to get his car fixed this week, or go down to Jamaica like she had been planning for six months? This wouldn't be the best time for him to remind her of when she forgot to disengage the emergency brake while she drove his car for three whole blocks two weeks earlier, or for her to tell him that perhaps she should go to Jamaica by herself since he hasn't been very interested in romance or any bedroom moves of late anyway. Even though this is the worst time for these accusations, it's when we often decide to make them.

Decisions around money are so absolutely fraught with tension and hostility that it often seems like we're in a no-win situation when these decisions have to be made. That's why both men AND women have to be extremely careful about how much they "assert" themselves on issues regarding money. We should consider ourselves walking on eggshells when the subject comes up, and so should you. Isn't it fascinating how much of our view of money and power comes from the things we saw in our parents' household as we were coming up? If we saw a single mother wielding the power, we males might have pledged that we would never again let a woman tell us what to do with our money. A black girl watching a single mother do the same things might have concluded that this is the way households are supposed to be run. If these two grow up and enter a relationship with each other— better duck! Money is going to be a topic they have to labor at with nonstop care, empathy and affection. It is NOT the time for somebody to be trying to "assert" something. That sounds like common sense, right? In fact, it is the situation most of us are in. We were raised in different households by different parents handling money in vastly different ways. So we all have vastly different expectations about money. When it comes to the cash, the watchword is *careful* . . . *careful*, and be as sensitive as possible.

Emotions: Can We Get Some?

From a Sistah

I've had a bad day, and my very best friend's gotten on my one good nerve with yet another teary tale about how she's leaving her trifling man? Oh—I'm going to tell you about it.

The cab driver wouldn't pick me up, so I missed my train, which means I won't get to see my mama for my much-needed rest and relaxation session—the one where I lay on the couch and sleep while she cooks up a panful of whiting and croakers and cornbread and grits? You can fully expect that I'm going to take special care to sit you down and explain detail for detail why I'm mad as all get-out.

You sent me flowers to the office, and then took me to a candlelit dinner at an expensive restaurant? After I finish hugging you and kissing you and thanking you, I'm going to tell you over and over again how sweet you are.

It's our nature—sistah nature—to tell you about it. We absolutely adore expressing our feelings, twirling thoughts and ideas and emotions around for discussion. We get off on it—Oprah's ratings should tell you that much.

Blame it on the way we raise little girls. We're told it's okay to express ourselves—to laugh and hug and smile when we're happy. We're encouraged, even when we grow up, to grin. If I had a nickel for every time some stranger told me, "You're so pretty—smile," or a dime for every time folks on my job or at church told me, "Why are you frowning? Just smile, honey," I'd be mugging for space on the front cover of *Forbes*.

The same goes for crying. How many of you have said to some poor little girl, "It's okay to cry, sweetie. Let it all out"?

Folks are always urging us to be emotional—telling us it's okay to show out. It's what girls do, and we play right into it, turn into these overly expressive creatures, these people who thrive on letting it all hang out. It's rare for us to keep anything inside—and if we do, sooner or later we'll burst with emotions anyway.

And whoever is on the receiving end of it? Watch out.

Shoot—thanks to sistahs and their emotions, AT&T, AOL and a whole host of therapists are paid in the shade.

But God forbid if we expect to get some unfettered feeling out of you brothers.

The boss blamed you for losing that account, knowing full well it was his fault?

Nothing from you.

It's storming outside and you can't get a cab because they just refuse to pick up your black butt?

You'll come home soaking wet, having walked 80 blocks to the subway—with not a word to say.

I call your mama a bitch?

Nothing.

I know that showing emotion has never been the brothers' strong suit. Sometimes we sistahs think you all would rather stand in front of a speeding Mack truck than let us know you're hurting, or that you don't have a situation under control. And Lord forbid if we're in an argument and we're looking for a fight. Shoot—get more rise out of a bucket of paint.

It's not like we're expecting you guys to cry every five minutes, or break down in a fit of rage if the soufflé isn't perfect, but stoicism seems to be the thing you guys grab for most when it comes to situations in which we sistahs think there's every reason to be emotional.

What's up with that? How come you all don't express yourselves and your feelings?

From a Brother

Do women really want a soft brother? I don't think so.

We hear this all the time, but we also hear a lot of other conflicting messages from women: "Oh, I don't want to go out with him, he's too nice." "Look at him (*pant, pant*). He's so sexy and masculine." Or, heard more recently, "He was crying just like a bitch."

Admit it, ladies, this stuff can easily confuse a brother. Especially if y'all are also confused. In certain situations, women seem to want their men as hard and strong and rock-solid as possible. You don't want to be strolling through the club with a man on your arm that you think other men and women are going to perceive as soft, right? You don't want to bring a man home to your father who's going to break down at the table and start complaining about how cruelly the world has been treating him, right?

Imagine this: A black man has had a hard day at work and he walks in the door to be greeted by his wife and two kids. He takes off his coat and gives his little one a hug. His wife asks him how the day went and he says: "Oh, my boss was so mean to me today, baby! I just can't take it anymore. He gave me a lot of work and he said really bad things to me." Then the man breaks down and starts sobbing.

I don't think there's a woman out there who would want her man to reveal that much emotion to the family. Families need fathers to provide stability and security, to give everyone proof that no matter how bad it gets on the outside, he's always going to be waiting back home to help you keep things together. If he looks like he's losing it, I think everyone loses it.

You might say these are extreme situations, but I only use them to make a point: There are times when women want us to be hard and there are times when they want us to be soft. But we have gotten so used to perfecting the hard that we don't know when and how to do the soft. If I show my soft side too early and start complaining to my new girlfriend that I can't seem to make sense of it all, there's a chance she might run away in terror because she doesn't know if this is a man she can rely on. And she might like to see me cry once in the first few months, but certainly not much more than that. Both men and women are still struggling with the definitions of masculinity. We think when women respond to the hard, unyielding male superstars they see on the big screen, like Clint Eastwood and Ving Rhames and Arnold Schwarzenegger and Denzel Washington, we are being told that we should act more like them. What that means to us is, give the world very little of yourself. Keep most of it buried inside and dole it out in explosive, tough little pieces. We think the opposite of these big-screen stars is Nathan Lane or Richard Simmons or Luther Vandross. Men who will give you tons of emotion. Men who are soft. We don't get to see many examples of a happy medium between the two after which to model ourselves.

It's clear that sistahs also feel like they need a hard exterior for the outside world. We see that every day when we try to walk up on the street and talk to a sistah-stranger without a résumé and five references in hand. So we men also have a guard that we think protects us from hurt. Often, the guard is there to send messages to other men. It's almost like animals pissing on trees to mark their territory. We think other men will assume they can dismiss and disrespect us if we don't look tough and hard. This starts as early as elementary school, when the class bully looks around the room in search of someone to pick on and you try to find your toughest look to scare him away—or at least show him you're not scared. Unfortunately, in many places black men have gotten to the point where they prey on each other, fighting for whatever little scraps are lying around. If you don't want another brother wandering over and trying to take what little you have managed to scrape together, you must project the hard guy exterior. In *Reaching up for Manhood,* author Geoffrey Canada presents a deeply affecting case about the fallacies of "manhood" that trap black men and cripple us. We have gotten very good at acting like the hard guy, but that's become the only way we know how to act.

If you want to try to help us, you must realize that being seen as weak and soft is what we're afraid of. A lot of black women can be brutally harsh and honest in assessing situations or someone else's character. It is often that harshness that scares us. We know black women encounter just as many obstacles or more during their workdays and have to find their own ways to deal with them, in addition to the gauntlet of rude, nasty black men who are all trying to chip away little pieces of the women on their commute home. So we think the last thing a black woman wants to hear about is the stresses and challenges we face. We think if we haven't learned to deal with these problems on our own, that makes us less of a man.

Of course you say you want to hear about all our problems so that we can struggle with them together and solve them together. That sounds wonderful. I wish we were able to lay it all on the table like that. But you might be grappling with the ghosts of old girlfriends who, instead of listening and quietly empathizing, thought we were bringing it up because we wanted our woman to tell us what to do. This is exactly what we do not want. We do not want our woman to solve our problems for us. Call it insecurity or ego if you want, but we need for the plan of action to be our own.

This may go all the way back to our mamas, who never hesitated to tell us what to do every chance they got. Eventually, we learned to stop bringing our problems to Mama because we grew tired of her lectures. I'm not blaming our mamas here—they were just doing what mamas do. But eventually the bird needs to fly on his own, and it's difficult for Mama to know when that time has arrived.

Dr. Gwendolyn Goldsby Grant, advice columnist for *Essence,* suggests that women start getting their men in the habit of talking about some of these difficult issues in the dark before you both fall asleep. She's right. Somehow it seems easier to talk about these things in the dark, when we don't have to worry about our women's examining eyes. And when you do it, the number one words of advice are: Don't Be Judgmental. Just Listen.

Though you talk about wanting an emotional man, aren't women also turned on by the image of strong, tough, stoic men of the type usually played by Clint Eastwood and Ving Rhames and Wesley Snipes?

From a Sistah

Stoicism, strength and heart are indeed traits that we love in brothers—and if it comes wrapped in a package like Ving Rhames or Wesley Snipes? Oh Lawdy, have mercy! But we don't want any of that brawn and sexiness to substitute for a man who expresses his emotions. Ideally, we'd like the entire package.

Let me break it down this way: When Ving Rhames won his Golden Globe award in 1998 for his spectacular and too-real-to-life portrayal of Don King in HBO's *Don King,* what did homeboy do? First, he reached over and kissed his wife. Then, as the tears gathered in his eyes, he squared his shoulders and took the long walk from his table to the stage, where, water running down his face, he talked about his love for the art of acting, happily accepted his award, then proudly handed it over to actor Jack Lemmon, whom Ving said deserved it more than he.

What's Ving? Like over six feet, well over two hundred pounds of strapping muscle? He's bald, he's big, he's black—and the characters he's played, from the evil, sadistic drug dealer Marcellus, in *Pulp Fiction,* to the strapping take-no-prisoners hero "Man" in John Singleton's *Rosewood,* add to his image as a really tough, strong, stoic kinda guy. But there he was, up on stage, crying like a baby.

And it was sexy as hell.

My sister-in-law and I talked about it for weeks afterward—how this big, strapping, muscle-bound man was strong enough to kiss his woman and cry his tears of joy for all the world to see. Trust me, the last thing Angelou and I thought after we saw that was, "Damn. Ving's one weak punk. Look at him, up there crying and stuff."

I say this to make this point: Strength and sensitivity are not mutually exclusive.

We are not going to think you any less of a man because you cried or laughed or you're melancholy or you needed a hug. In fact, we'll think you more of a man—because you're mature enough to be secure enough in your manhood to know that no real woman is going to cut you off for showing her a little emotion.

In fact, it was this, in part, that attracted me to my husband. One evening while we were hanging at his house, he was listening to his answering machine when he heard what he considered terrible news: His ex-wife had found a new job and was moving away with their son to another city. Nick was bothered by the idea of not living in the same house with his child, but he was comforted by the fact that his ex-wife lived just a short distance away from his Brooklyn home. The news that his child would be so far away that he'd likely have to cut down his visits to once or twice a month was heart-wrenching for him—and he cried, right there in front of me. It was not pleasurable for me to see him cry. But that he felt so strongly for his son—that he loved him so that the mere thought of having this child removed from his world—was endearing. So often we get the notion that men just sort of have kids, pat them on the head when they come home from work, and hand the credit card over when Mommy wants to buy new clothes for Junior. Rarely do we get the images that help us recognize that fathers are just as emotionally attached to their children as mothers are. To see this man crying over his child told me a lot about him: that he was—and is—a good, loving father; that he has feelings and respected our relationship—and me—enough to let me know that he was hurting; and that he knew that he was still a man after his last tear had dried. "Oh, look at him, he's crying just like a bitch," never once crossed my mind.

I'm sure there are a lot of sistahs out there who feel the same way.

Now, that doesn't mean we need you up in the house crying like a baby every time some stuff goes down. You're absolutely right in saying that no woman honestly wants a soft brother who copes by crying every chance he gets. When we sistahs do that, you think us needy—and we'd feel the same way about a man who did it. And we certainly don't need a man who will take advantage of us by crying his way out of trouble (you know who you are).

But a man who is strapping and strong and sweet and has a heart?

Watch out.

I wonder, though, does the fact that we express our emotions ever turn guys off?

From a Brother

Most men are a little afraid of women who are too needy. An overly needy woman is a "taker." She will take so much that she won't ever have time to even think about giving. Where's the fun in that?

We all cherish the idea of providing our women with emotional support, being the solid shoulder to lean on in our women's times of need. But we don't want you all to get carried away. We'd also like to know that you have your stuff together, that you are strong enough to make it through your days in that cold world without hovering daily on the verge of a breakdown. Of course, we don't want the other extreme, either—that is, the superwoman who will tell anyone who will listen (and even those who don't want to hear it) that she doesn't NEED anyone, least of all a man. We want to stay away from her, too.

If a man is ready to start looking for the future mother of his children, he's seeking some stability. We become afraid that if we walk down the aisle with an emotionally needy woman, she might lose it at the wrong time and leave us with a family to raise by ourselves after we send her off somewhere to unravel out of the sight of the children. Good mothers are not overly needy. Good wives are not overly needy.

How do you know if you're too emotionally needy? Well, if you think you might be, then you probably are. In other words, if it's something that you spend a fair amount of time worrying about, then you likely realize your neediness has gotten out of hand. If you need daily reassurance from your man that he . . .

> loves you,
> thinks you're pretty,
> doesn't think you're fat,
> thinks you're smart,
> doesn't think you're ditzy,
> desires you,
> doesn't think you ask him too many questions,

then you should think about employing the services of someone who will love your neediness—for at least $100 an hour.

It's all about moderation, baby (to partially steal a phrase from Puff Daddy). We know you have plenty of emotions to share and we want to hear them and see them, but not all at once and not right away. In the movie *Broadcast News,* Holly Hunter's character has to have a good long cry every night before she goes to sleep. If that's you, it would be wise to go out in the back yard to do it for at least the first year of the relationship if you don't want to send the man screaming into the night.

Even if we are about as stable as a rabid dog, we try to avoid women who we think will require too much work. Some guys refer to these women as "high-maintenance."

High maintenance makes you walk around your own house on eggshells, for fear that your woman will think you don't love her anymore because you closed the door when you took a dump.

High maintenance means she blows her top if you break off the post-sex cuddle after four minutes and thirty seconds instead of the requisite five minutes.

High maintenance requires a phone call to her office every afternoon at 3:00 P.M. to tell her you miss her.

High maintenance mandates that you hold her hand in the mall at least once every thirty minutes.

High maintenance is a pain in the ass.

You should also try to read your man's moods. If he pulls you close and keeps you enveloped in a tight embrace, he might be in a mood to see some of your emotion. That might be a good time to tell him that you hate your . . . job, mother, hair, boss, father, butt, sister, breasts, brother, kneecaps, nose hair, house, halitosis, best friend, apartment—you get the idea. If, however, he has just pulled a beer from the six-pack, which he has conveniently moved to the front of the refrigerator in front of the orange juice, he has fluffed the pillows behind his back, he has carefully arranged the *Sports Illustrated*s at his feet to read during the commercials, and he has just clicked on the seventh game of the NBA finals, do everyone a favor—don't share, okay? It's not a good time. And if you can't recognize this, you need to be sent back to the factory for realignment, because something's out of whack.

Romance: How Can We Get Some?

From a Sistah

The brother's been teasing her all day long—done told her that this evening will be unlike any other she's ever experienced before. "Just you wait, baby—a night you will not forget," he coos into the phone. Every hair on her neck stands on end; she's writhing in her seat, running the white hanky across her brow.

Not two milliseconds after she's hung up with her man, sis is on the phone calling every last one of her girlfriends, telling them if they hear some howling 'round midnight, when the moon is full, that's her man—Brother Mr. Romance—turning her out. She's already pictured the scene: He will show up in a beautiful tailored suit, smelling like Cool Water, a beautiful bouquet of roses peeking from behind his back. He will gingerly place her hand in his, and lead her to the ride—open the door for her, and close it behind her, too—and whisk her away to a romantic moonlit picnic on the boardwalk, overlooking the water and the magnificent city skyline. And then he will take her chin in his hand, and guide her lips to his, and the passion of their kiss will light a thousand stars.

And then 8:00 P.M. rolls around, and homeboy rings her doorbell and he's standing there on her doorstep with a bucket of Kentucky Fried and a six-pack of Heineken and *Terminator* I and II and a big-ass grin. "Girl, don't tell me I don't know how to plan a romantic evening!" he charges as he pushes his way over to the living room and plops his greasy, dusty sneaker-and-jean-clad butt on her good couch. "Where's the remote?"

Then it all comes rushing back to you: Flowers are the beginning and end of romance for him, Arnold Schwarzenegger his Friday-night love god. This boy ain't seen this side of romantic since before Billy Dee started wrapping his hands around the Colt 45s. You want romantic? He lets you flip over to the Lifetime channel while he takes a popcorn/bathroom/beer-run break. And, um, make sure Arnold's back on the screen by the time booty connects with sofa, thank you.

An all too familiar story, ladies?

It's as if God stockpiled us with this yearning for romance, and then thought it would be a great goof to, like, forget to put the romance gene in our mates. One of us craves it; the other treats it like the bubonic plague.

Then we walk around with our mouths poked out, wondering if we've already settled into, like, this old married couple thing. I mean, he started off on the right foot with flowers on the first date, a romantic dinner on the second, a sweet stroll through the park on the third. But by the fourth? Movie, burger, back seat—movie, burger, back seat.

There has to be more to this—some occurrence that snaps you brothers out of your desire to please. Perhaps some kind of manual somewhere that we sistahs don't know about, one that dictates that you all drop romance like a bad habit early so, you know, we don't get used to it or something.

Perhaps you can help us out: Why can't you all be more romantic?

From a Brother
This is an area where we truly need some help sometimes.

You dis us for thinking that buying some flowers is the height of romance, but flowers is one of the few lessons that the world has bothered to pass along to us on what qualifies as romance. There are several factors that make this whole subject a lot more complicated than it needs to be:

1. Every woman's idea of romance is a little different. While sandwiches and a picnic basket might make us James Bond–smooth in the eyes of one cutie, another might not think the word "romance" should even be used until we spend half the total of our paycheck. So with these wires crossing in our heads about even the basic definition of romance, we are sometimes a little paralyzed and unsure of what to do. For many of us, our idea of romance comes from the movies or—even worse—our friends. In all likelihood, these are not the world's best role models. Should we try imitating Eddie Murphy's Marcus charac-ter in *Boomerang*—you know, the gourmet meals, the unbelievably phat apartment, the silky-smooth lines? If you say "Yes," then many of us need to go out and find a $200,000-a-year job first in order to afford all that smoothness. Okay, flowers not enough? How about we add some candles on the table? My friend Willie used to tell me y'all liked that. But I suspect that candles might be as played as flowers. See? From where are we supposed to find a clue?

2. If we've only got, like, two or maybe three ideas of a romantic evening, how eager are we likely to be to keep repeating the same tired gimmick every month? Even if we alternate the expensive restaurant with the lavish meal we cooked with our own hands, we figure somewhere in the middle of the rest of our lives you're going to get tired of our version of romance. So what do we do? Mostly, nothing. Back to the paralysis.

Just as you might suspect, one reason we aren't more romantic is that we get lazy. It's not that we don't *like* romance, it's just that we've always kinda looked at it as a means to an end—if you catch my drift. In the middle of the romantic interlude, we tingle just as much as the woman—but it's more like a tingle of anticipation, not a tingle from the romance itself. If the poontang is going to be forthcoming whether we go for the romance or just go straight for the titties, after a while many of us start skipping the romance part. Why waste time with setting a mood, putting on music, lighting the candles, or whatever else we might have tried early in the relationship when we have that delectable body beckoning to us? The sight of a lighted candle doesn't send us into paroxysms of sighs and "ooohs" unless we know it's gonna lead to something. You see our predicament? We start taking you and the sex for granted because we can get it without a whole lot of work. But before you start trashing us for our laziness, think about this:

It's 11:30. You have been home for two hours because you had to work late. You ate at about 10:00 and you're still feeling a little bloated and sluggish. You're tired as hell because you've been going in early to finish a difficult project. Are you really in the mood for romance?

Or: It's 10:30 and you smell like vomit because your one-year-old just deposited his dinner on your shirt. You're smelling a bit florid from chasing the four-year-old around the house to give her a bath, and your mate has already fallen asleep on the couch because he or she didn't get any sleep the night before after the one-year-old woke up at 3:00 A.M. wanting somebody to play with him. Romance? Maybe with your pillow.

We want and need some clues from you about what we should do and when we should do it. Maybe there is something we can cook up to make you come alive at 11:30 after you've been working late once again. Or after you've put the kids to bed and you have vomit on that old raggedy T-shirt.

But a word of caution: We might be a little defensive about our cluelessness. After all, we suspect that you think we're romanceless clods; therefore, the last thing we want to hear from you is that we're romanceless clods. So what you do is use the same kind of positive reinforcement that you use with your kids. Or your nieces and nephews, or your neighbor's kids. Instead of, "Hey, moron, next time use the china behind the glass with the spotlight on it instead of the paper plates," try, "Darling, you're so romantic; I just love it when you cook for me [or go to the gourmet food store and buy such delicious takeout]. It would be even more wonderful the next time if you used the beautiful dishes my parents gave us when we got married." Instead of, "Hey, retard, couldn't you at least look at me or, God forbid, give me a kiss the next time you pick me up from work?" try, "I love it when you pick me up from work, honey, because it shows me that you've missed me during the day as much as I've missed you. It would be even more wonderful if you surprised me one day and picked me up in a horse-drawn carriage so we could ride through the park."

In other words, bury the romance suggestions inside a compliment instead of smacking us in the face with them. There's a chance some of us still won't catch on at first, but even the most romance-phobic of us might eventually be moved if we get enough of this stuff.

Sometimes, though, I wonder if women don't get just a little suspicious if we seem a bit too romantic, or always have the perfect words for every situation. **If we come with too much of this romance stuff in the beginning, won't your "playa" alarm start whooping loud enough to wake the whole neighborhood?**

From a Sistah

Show up with flowers, and we'll think it's just the sweetest thing. Show up with flowers two days after you stood us up, with yet another sorry excuse for why you didn't call, or why you didn't write, or why you just didn't, and hell, yeah, we're going to look for the leash—because it's going to be quite obvious that Mr. Snoop Puppy Pup needs to be untied and left to roam with the rest of the doggies out in the wild.

See, we don't need—or want—the romance without the feelings behind it.

No, there's nothing sweeter than the smell of a fresh bouquet of spring flowers, placed gingerly on the corner of your desk at the job—nothing more utterly delicious than a sumptuous dinner by candlelight, served up by our man's hands. Hell, it could be a bucket of chicken and a daisy on the hood of the car in the parking lot in the middle of the afternoon—it's just as sweet and delicious and tender.

But only if it's sincere.

We need to know—and the brothers need to show—that the flowers and the candy and the candlelight and the bubble baths are the sweet companions of a budding romance, the fringe benefits of a relationship that has possibilities. We want you to take us for that romantic stroll on the beach because you want to, not because you think it's a necessary task you need to carry out if it means we'll climb into the sack with you.

And don't think we can't spot the guys who are playing us like ole boy did in *Boomerang*. Our radars can spot that cheap, plastic-encased rose you picked up from the bum at the red light around the corner—you know, the brother who dug his stash out of the garbage after the florist put out the day's trash—quicker than diva model Naomi Campbell can root out a two-dollar sharkskin suit on an Armani runway. It may take us a minute to figure out we're getting played, but eventually, your gig will be exposed—and up.

Of course, you could help us out a bit here if you let us in on this little secret: How can we more quickly tell that a brother's romantic gestures aren't sincere?

From a Brother

*You want me to reveal the prized, hidden secrets of the playa trade?
Those invaluable silky-smooth steps that brothers have perfected to
make the **Kama Sutra** look like it was written by Fred Sanford?*

Well, I could tell you, but then I'll have to kill you.

I don't want to make us sound like we are incapable of looking five minutes into the future, but . . . uh, we usually start thinking about romantic gestures when we're on our way to pick you
up, or as the car is pulling into the garage, or as we're turning off
the lights, or as we're sliding in . . . In other words, we usually
think of gestures as a way to enhance whatever it is we hope will
follow them. Is that sincere or insincere?

Somewhere in the back of our heads, there's always a distant
voice telling us to think of something romantic or kind to do for
our woman. We aren't usually sure of what that thing is until it
smacks us in the face. So unless we have committed some heinous
relationship crime and are begging for leniency from the judge,
we're not likely to turn up the volume of that distant voice often
enough to satisfy our ladies. If we happen to be in the mall buying
a new case of tennis or golf balls, getting a racquet restrung, or
some socks (we always need socks), and we make a wrong turn
and stumble into a jewelry store, then it might occur to us that a
romantic or kind thing would be to buy you a piece of jewelry.
We'll check our watches, calculate that we have at least thirteen
minutes to spare, look helplessly at one of those nice middle-aged
salesladies draped in gaudy, sparkling pieces, and ask what they
got for under $100 that would make our wife/girlfriend very

happy. The saleslady will smile broadly at us and compliment us on being so romantic, not knowing the romance was truly the consequence of a miscalculation about which corridor led to the parking garage. She'll lead us to the necklaces/bracelets/earrings, we'll snatch up one that's not too cheap but not too expensive, either, then we'll hit the house and feel like a hero for the rest of the night—particularly later in the bedroom. At these moments, it will occur to us that this romance thing isn't that hard at all, and it certainly is worth it to see the smile on your face, but then tomorrow will come and the voice way back in our head will tell us that we better think of something pretty damn good the next time because it'll be pretty hard to top jewelry—and certainly jewelry is now out of the question for at least another six to ten months.

Sincere or insincere? You make the call.

In other words, for most of us, this romantic stuff doesn't come naturally. It requires thought, foresight, deep attention to details. If a brother seems to have such a firm grasp on the romantic gesture that eventually you're tempted to peek behind his back to see if he's consulting a manual, than your playa alarm should start a making some noise. If you're still not sure, you could always buy some sunglasses and a wig and follow his behind.

Division of Labor:
Can Ya Help Me?

From a Sistah

It's not easy being a nineties woman.

Not that our mamas had it easy, what with the circumstances of the forties and fifties and sixties, when times were so hard that she had to get on her knees over in the white folks' house to scrub the floors and the toilets and wipe the noses of their snot-nosed kids, then come home to fry the chicken and keep house and wipe Junior's snotty nose while Daddy was out trying to rustle up enough money to help keep the family living. But today? No doubt it's still hard to be a working woman with a family.

We have high-powered careers that are just as demanding as those maintained by men; the boss demands just as much from us as he does from Bill; we're expected to work long hours and put in as much overtime and sacrifice our whole selves to the company altar. Yet we still don't get paid as much as men, we still don't get the same promotional opportunities and we damn sure don't get the same recognition as men, either.

And when we come home, it's just as uneven. If we've got kids, we're rushing in the morning to get them dressed and fed and off to the baby-sitter or to school, and we're rushing in from the job to feed them, get them to soccer practice, ballet lesson and choir rehearsal, help them with their homework, and usher them off to bed. Then we're cleaning up the dishes and straightening up after everybody and, all at the same time, trying to finish up that project that we have to hand in at work.

Our mates? Well, they're working hard—at their careers. They sort of saunter in after a hard day's work, pat Junior on the head, talk to him for a few minutes—on a good night, he might even play with him—head over to the table for some grub, then retire to the study to either do more work or have a cold beer while they watch the game.

On Fridays, they'll change it up a little bit by letting us see the paycheck before they deposit it into the joint account.

I certainly don't have to tell you about the fathers who don't live with their babies and their mamas, the checkbook daddies. You know the type—the ones who think their fatherly responsibilities are fulfilled when they lick the stamp and drop the child support in the mail. We can all sum up their laborial participation in three words: Absolutely no help.

And I won't even get on the Negroes who drop babies from here to Kalamazoo and do absolutely nothing for their former lovers except give her a reason to find herself on the welfare line—and demonized by every neoconservative-pull-yourself-up-by-your-bootstraps politician using welfare reform to make their own career advances.

Certainly, none of the above makes it any easier for the nineties woman, who's juggling career and family and trying to keep her head above water. No, not every man is like the three mentioned above; there are some good brothers out there who recognize their responsibility to keep the scales balanced when their woman is working just as hard as they are during the day. And yes, men are definitely contributing way more when it comes to childrearing and housekeeping than they did when, say, my dad first married. We certainly won't knock the ones who are bringing home a nice share of the bacon. But a sobering statistic by *Ms.* magazine recently pointed out this fact: Men are still contributing only a paltry 20 percent to the household and child-rearing chores in our homes. You don't have to be a mathematician to see that brothers and sistahs are far from equal when it comes to taking care of our kids and home.

One would think that this would have changed by now.

What's going on? How come men think that putting money into the bank account is their sole contribution when it comes to the division of household and child-rearing responsibilities?

From a Brother

Remember when your mom used to come to your room to inspect your supposed cleanup effort and always find fifteen things you forgot to do? Well, that's the situation men are in when it comes to housework and child rearing—there's always going to be fifteen more things we could have done.

We'd be all right if at the start of every month, the man and the woman could sit down and list every single thing that would need to get done around the house over the next thirty-one days. Then we could put exactly half the items on one side of the page and the other half on the other side. We could flip a coin to see who got the right side and who got the left side. Then, as the weeks progressed, we could check off items as we completed them and know we were doing exactly half our share. But housework and child rearing don't work like that. Every day of the week presents a whole new set of responsibilities and must-do items that we could never have anticipated the night before. And we just don't seem to be as adept as our female counterparts at identifying each of these tasks before they're screaming up in our face.

We got Tarik dressed and fed him breakfast before school; we're feeling pretty good about our contributions to the household. But we neglected to ask him whether he had any papers or forms that we were supposed to sign and return to school. We forgot to tell him to remind his teacher he'd be leaving early because he has a dentist's appointment that afternoon—to which he is being carted by Mom, who will have to deal with the teacher's annoyance. We didn't look up at the sky or read the paper to see that it'd be raining later that afternoon and Tarik would need a rain slicker.

In her book *A Natural History of Parenting: A Naturalist Looks at Parenting in the Animal World and Ours,* science writer Susan Allport points out that the role of men in child rearing has long been underplayed in our society. Going out and earning a living to provide food, shelter and security to a family may not be as directly crucial to an offspring's survival as a mother's milk and minute-to-minute nurturing, but the child wouldn't thrive without the father's contribution, which is no different than that of many of the males in the animal kingdom, who go find food and protect their nest from predators. As has been well documented, the problem has cropped up in our society as women's opportunities in the workplace have increased quicker than the male's contributions to the workload at home. Many of us want to do more or as much as our spouses, but we feel that we can never do enough to make the thing look split down the middle until we develop the ability to read our women's minds. That way, we'd know when she felt something needed to be done as soon as the thought crossed her mind.

Often, the kind of work we take responsibility for around the house just *looks* different than the work our women do. If I take two days to replace a sink in the basement bathroom, my mate will have done no less than fifty separate child-rearing and houseworking tasks to my one. She might be happy to have a new sink in the basement, but in her mind it'll take me about two months to catch up to her fifty tasks. Of course, during those two months, she will have done about two hundred other things that I haven't matched. After a decade of marriage, her lead could be in the thousands—and she could be getting increasingly pissed with each passing year. What needs to happen to prevent her from getting pissed is for the two of us to talk about our respective household tasks *before* we undertake them so that the male can get a better handle on what his woman wants and whether she thinks things are being fairly divided.

Recent news reports suggest that things are getting better.

Men are doing much more around the house. We now spend about 73 percent of the time on household tasks that women do (according to a recent study by the Families and Work Institute), while we spend three-quarters of the time our women do with the kids. Still far from fifty–fifty, but we're getting there. I know we do a lot more than our fathers did; our kids likely will do much more than us. Seventy-five years down the line, my great-great-granddaughter's going to have a hubby who shares the tasks in their house exactly fifty–fifty. Maybe she'll be happy with him. But then she'll wake up the next morning and realize he forgot to pick up her black suit from the cleaners. She wanted to wear that suit to work.

If we need for you to tell us when and what you want us to do—in other words, if our sixth sense about household and child-rearing chores isn't as well developed as yours—will it ever seem to you like we're sharing 50 percent of the household responsibilities?

From a Sistah

We don't want to have to tell you to help us with the child-rearing and household chores; we simply want you to recognize you should be pitching in and, like Nike, just do it.

It's not rocket science—you don't need a master's degree to figure it out. We need help around the house and we need help with the kids, way more than most men are willing to or think they have to give. We bring home the bacon after ten hours on the job, we fry it in the pan for you and Junior every night and we never, ever let you forget you're a man—lest we be accused of being cold fish—and we get no credit and absolutely no glory for doing it.

For those of us sistahs with kids and a career, it's no joke. Junior needs to be awakened in the morning, his teeth need brushing, he needs to be dressed, he needs to be fed, he needs to go to school with all his homework in his bag, he needs to be cuddled and held and told he's the best kid in the world and he needs to be seen off to school—all before 7:30 A.M. Then I have to go to work, deal with "the man" all day long, come home tired and frustrated, pick Junior up from school, cart him off to soccer practice, act like I've got enough energy to cheer him on, cart him back home, feed him and you, help him with his homework, bathe him, cuddle him some more, and tuck him in the bed.

Your grand contribution? While I'm busting the suds from tonight's dinner, you're reading Junior a bedtime story.

Whoa! Hold back now—be careful not to bust a gut with all that help.

For those of us sistahs who don't have kids, it's all the same; we work, then come home to a man who's waiting to be fed and bedded, somewhere between us taking care of most—if not all—of the household responsibilities.

It used to be easy for brothers to argue what Susan Allport does—that the man is fulfilling his familial responsibilities by providing for and protecting his family. But that argument just doesn't hold water these days, not with sistahs working just as hard as and, in some cases, earning just as much as or more than their male counterparts. One would think that just as we started taking on more of the so-called man roles in the relationship—earning the loot and fiercely protecting the family—that the men would have assumed some of the so-called womanly responsibilities—the nurturing and taking care of home thang.

Alas, that's not happening enough—and, all too often, not at all.

In a perfect world, you would know that I toiled just as hard at work today as you did, you would understand my plight in having to balance that tiredness with my child care and household responsibilities and you would—no, not offer to help—dig in without me asking.

What a concept! A man who sees the dirty dishes in the sink and washes them, knows Junior needs his teeth brushed at night and brushes them, knows we all have to eat dinner when we come home in the evening and cooks, knows we ran out of eggs and cereal and he just drank the last drop of milk and goes grocery shopping—just knows.

But it just doesn't work that way with you all, does it? A woman who participated in a *Sistahs' Rules* forum with me in Philadelphia explained it perfectly when she said she was raised by her single father and understood the ways of men. She told us that she could go for days without milk to put into her cereal because her father would simply forget to buy it. It wasn't that he didn't love her or that he was neglectful or that he didn't care about his baby having cereal for breakfast; he just didn't think about simple things like buying milk, the sistah said. He needed her to tell him, "Daddy, we need milk," for him to actually get to the grocery store. He'd go without delay, but he still needed to be told.

Frankly, we just don't get that. We're not asking you to read our minds on this one; we're simply telling you that if you drink the last glass of milk, go buy some—damn. If you know Junior plays soccer on Tuesdays and Thursdays, tell me you'll pick him up on Tuesday if I pick him up on Thursday. If you know the laundry needs to be done and you're down to your last pair of drawers—the ones with the hole in the wrong place and the jacked-up elastic waistband—dammit, do the laundry. Don't sit around waiting on me to do it.

Just do it.

I have to admit that it does make it a bit easier when we lay down some ground rules on what we expect from you. For instance, Nick and I have an unspoken rule regarding cooking: If I cook, he washes dishes, and vice versa. And if we're both hungry, he has no problem cooking dinner, which is way cool. He's also very good with his son, Mazi, whom he feeds, bathes, clothes and reads to when he's at our house—which told me a whole lot about what kind of father Nick will be when we have some crumb-snatchers of our own. He has no problem doing laundry, he's no stranger to the grocery store, and when the apartment needs straightening up, he's just as likely to be on the case as I am, if not more.

Most women aren't so lucky. Indeed, it's hard not to wonder if men are just happy with the status quo—if their refusal to buy the milk or change Junior's diapers or vacuum the carpet at least twice in the next millennium is their own quiet revelation: Brothers want sistahs to fry the chicken and wipe Junior's snotty little nose because that's what his mama did for his daddy, and that's what women are supposed to do for men. **In fact, most sistahs would venture to say that brothers want their women to simply take care of them. Is that the case?**

From a Brother

The only time most modern brothers expect a sistah to take care of us is for about a week after the industrial accident. But after the week is up and we learn to dress ourselves with the nubs, we'll be back on our own.

This just doesn't enter into our expectations anymore—not if we're gonna be chillin' with a working woman. If a brother is going into a relationship in the new millennium with the anticipation that he's going to come home every night to a home-cooked meal, a back and foot massage and a compliant sexual partner, he's going to be out on the street so fast that he won't even have time to grab his coat.

Though we know we're expected to do our share, many of us have never been properly trained for the role. In households that contain little boys and girls, our mothers still place more of the domestic chores in the girls' hands, letting the boys stand by while the girls learn how to do the things that will keep them alive as adults. Twenty years ago my mother made me do just as many household chores as my sisters did. While I didn't like it at the time, I think it made me more willing as a man to grab a pot and pan and give it a go in the kitchen, or take a rag and start scrubbing in the bathroom. I hate to blame yet another of our shortcomings on Mom, but that's where it needs to start. Mothers, shove that boy into the kitchen, hand him a cookbook, and try to ignore the crashes and screams in the kitchen area for the next few hours.

I'd venture a guess that many men probably would like it if their women cooked for them a bit more, but most would submit to a CIA interrogation before they'd actually tell them. That's because we're already made to feel as if we're the laziest, least deserving creatures on the planet—not only our mates but our society likes reminding us of this. That's certainly the consistent theme used to sell beer on television. Remember the one about the guys sitting around and drinking brew as they laughed about the dummies they had placed in strategic places in their homes to make their wives think they were doing repairs rather than sitting up in a bar? It was pretty funny the first two hundred times I saw it, but then I realized what it was saying: Men don't want to help their wives; they spend all of their time trying to avoid helping their wives; the cleverest prototypes of the species will go so far as to trick their wives to get out of doing their fair share. What's my son supposed to think when he sees that? What pain will he put himself and some unsuspecting female through thirty years from now because this silly commercial and a thousand others with similar messages have been replayed in his subconscious in a continuous closed-end loop throughout his developing years?

What needs to happen is we need to sit down with each other once a month, once a week, once a year, whatever seems to work best and cause the least amount of enmity, and divide up those damn chores. No way around it.

Hit the Road, Jack: Knowing When to Say "Enough"

From a Sistah

We hate to do it, but we'll get around to it eventually.

And when we do it?

Whoo.

It just takes most of us more than a little bit of time to get there, that's all. We'll see all the signs that tell us the relationship is dead and stinking—they come at us like those yellow neon signs warning cars that a curve is coming up in the roadway—but we will ignore each and every one of them like the plague because we figure almost any love thang can get fixed.

He could have been sleeping in the next room, hasn't touched us since the last child was conceived, forgot how to form the words "I love you" on his lips—or, worse yet, figured out how to say them to someone else—and we will give it just one more shot, because we swore before God, our mama and all our big-mouthed girlfriends that this was going to last through real thick, real thin and the wake, and damn if we're going to give up all we built with you, forget all the feelings we had for you, leave everything that our relationship was behind, because things aren't working out today.

We'll also hold on because it was hard as hell getting you and we're not particularly keen on getting back into the dating scene again—especially while we have a broken heart.

But then there just comes a point when you got to know when to say, "Enough already," and walk away. We may take a while longer, but we get there. **How about brothers: Are men more willing to leave a relationship when they feel it's not working, even though they've invested a lot of time in it?**

From a Brother

As the relationship stumbles and lurches toward its final days and it's obvious the life-support tubes should be pulled, both parties are usually closely watching the other, playing the Who Will Drop the Ax? game. In these situations, I think brothers aren't willing to wait as long as sistahs before going ahead and wielding that ax.

Logistically, this means the women will wait us out, often cutting off all the supply lines (no sex, no romance, little conversation, certainly no smiles) that provide us with the things we need from a relationship. So there we are, feeling emotionally and physically detached, wondering why we're even in her presence anymore if she's going to pretend we don't exist. If this goes on long enough, we're going to start looking elsewhere for the relationship sustenance we want and need. Once we have found someone else or the iciness has become just too unpleasant to bear, we will take a deep breath and begin the proceedings to Drop the Ax.

Dropping the Ax is one of the least pleasant things that a man or a woman has to do in life. That's why both sides try to avoid it as long as they can, even if they both know it's necessary for everyone's sanity and safety. Speaking of safety, this might be a reason why many women are afraid to Drop the Ax themselves— they're involved with a psychopath who's capable of pulling out a firearm if they threaten to leave. (Why else would there be so many battered women's shelters all over the land?) But I think these losers constitute a tiny fraction of the brothers in bad relationships—at least, I hope they do.

The desire to avoid the Dropping the Ax conversation might lead some brothers to make one of the biggest mistakes they can at this delicate time—become involved with another woman before you end the bad relationship. Sure, the brother may feel as if he has all the justification in the world—"Hey, SHE ended the relationship when she stopped sleeping with me," he might tell anyone who will listen—but once he strays and gets busted, THAT will become precisely the catalyst his woman needs to call him a lyin', cheatin' dog and tell all her friends that's why she threw him out. How much better a case brotherman would have had in asserting his claim of physical and emotional non-interest if he had waited until the dust had cleared before he started getting that interest from somewhere else.

If both sides can manage to come together and achieve one of those rare consensual ax droppings, they'll both be able to tell friends that things just "didn't work out." Hell, they could even do the Seinfeld and Elaine thing and remain close friends. That's difficult when things have become so unpleasant that you'd prefer never to see the person again in life, but if both sides are proactive enough in spotting the rotting fruit before the stink blankets the room, the man and the woman have a chance to walk away with no bloodshed and maybe even no tears—though that's probably even rarer than the consensual ax dropping.

Brothers usually have a harder time with these consensual ax droppings than sistahs. If there's not gonna be any more sex, what's the point in staying friends? To talk? I'm joking slightly, but that is the way many men feel.

When things are starting to look a little bumpy, what are the signs sistahs look for to determine whether a relationship is heading for the rocks? When do you decide you've had ENOUGH?

From a Sistah

You asked for it, you got it. This is how to tell when enough is enough:

- You start referring to him as "what's-his-name."
- The box of condoms in the drawer has passed the expiration date because they've been sitting there for so long.
- He'd rather watch porno movies than have sex. Come to think of it, you would, too.
- You don't even bother running into the bathroom anymore when you need to fart around him.
- You start developing a peculiar fascination with the Lorena Bobbitt story—and you start dreaming about Vienna sausages.

• When he smacks you on the behind during sex, you turn around and smack him in the face.

• When you go out to dinner together, he asks for separate tables.

• He doesn't even hesitate to tell you you're fat.

• Though he feigns ignorance, you wonder how the screws got removed from the guardrail on your apartment balcony.

But tell me, if a brother Drops the Ax, is there a chance for a reconciliation—or is it just over in his mind?

From a Brother

This is where brothers are sometimes hurt by their lack of memory of relationship details, particularly years later. When an old flame steps back into our lives and she's looking hot and sexy, we might have forgotten all the things we hated about her and why we got out in the first place. If she looks even better than she did before, we might not even remember how we got the scar across our forehead and the velocity homegirl can get on her fastball when she directs the ashtray at a male skull.

In an ideal world, we'd remember every detail about every relationship sin that every woman ever committed against us. But this ain't even close to an ideal world and we have a hard time recalling her parents' names, never mind the way she farted in her sleep and called out the names of other dudes as she climaxed. I think we should carry index cards around with us and write down the details of every argument we have with our mates—in addition to the perfume she likes, her dress size and her ring size. We could keep the cards in a small file cabinet that we lock up in a vault—so new women in our lives can't snoop around in there. Then when an old flame steps back to the plate, we'd have every detail we'd ever need about her and why she's now an EX-girlfriend. We might even store all this information on a laptop computer so it's more readily available to us. That way, if we met the old flame at a party or in a grocery store, before we made a huge mistake and asked her out for drinks, we could run back to our car and call up her file—and then drive home as fast as our wheels will take us.

If we were the ones to Drop the Ax, then we had definite reasons for it. If we remember any of them a few years down the line, it's unlikely we'd want to take the risk of putting ourselves through possible pain all over again. Sure, she might have reformed, perhaps she doesn't break into tears anymore if we fail to tell her we love her at the end of every phone conversation—but there's just too much at stake to risk it. On the outside, she might appear to be a thoroughly different person. You go out a few times, you remember how nice it was between the sheets, you recall how much you liked the curve of her back—then you come home one day and find her sitting in front of a table covered with empty Dunkin' Donuts boxes and you remember the binges that put you over the edge.

In two words, NO RECONCILIATION. We usually think it's a bad idea.

Perhaps I should add a few caveats here. I believe that women with whom we had flings in high school, college or soon after college probably deserve a second look later on down the line because there's no way of predicting how they're going to turn out when we're still young and clueless. Life does interesting things to people, turning that college doormat into Naomi Campbell or the confused, indecisive sophomore into a beautiful, confident senior executive ten years later. I had an older friend who once advised me to never be too mean or dismissive of the stupid, ugly girls in high school and college because you never knew what plans Mother Nature had for them later on. Of course, it wasn't my style to be mean or dismissive—but the advice didn't hurt.

Keeping It New: How Concerned Are We with Keeping It Hot, Hot, Hot?

From a Sistah

Yeah, I used to call you every hour on the hour at work and e-mail you every half-hour between, just to say, "I love you," or hear your voice, or ask you something silly, like, "What you doing?" when I knew full well you were making that money. And you'd gleefully await my call—know it was me, and I knew you knew it was me, because you'd answer with that "Hey, baby" voice, deep and sexy and seductive, and on the first ring.

Now, I don't even know your work number—and when I do manage to find it, I get your secretary, who tells me you'll get back to me as soon as you can. And you don't because you know you'll see me at home any ol' way.

Used to rush home from work and set candles up all around the house and turn on that Maxwell cee-dee nice and soft and low and slip into that new sexy, stringy nightie I bought just for this occasion—which isn't a special occasion, mind you, just an end-of-the-day occasion—and spread myself like butter across the satin sheets in our bedroom, anxiously awaiting the connection of key metal to lock metal and your foot to floor, every step toward me making me breathe that much harder and faster until you darkened the doorway.

Now? Flannel, knee-length jersey nightie, socks with pom-poms, slippers, curlers, night cream and a magazine. I'm watching the TV here—take your beer and your burping and your holey drawers into the living room, please, and close the door all the way when you leave, thank you.

Used to use up those vacation days damn near before the year hit its midpoint—but not with weeklong vacations to exotic beaches anywhere. Oh, no—they were used on every Thursday, Friday and Monday between January and June, on days we spent traveling to every bed and breakfast on this side of the Mason-Dixon line, just getting away from the boss and the traffic and the noise and the phone ringing and everything else that can distract us from each other just to be with one another—in each other's arms—simply content.

Now the vacation days are taken the same time every year—the week of the kids' spring break, the first week in July, when the kids get out of school and Christmas—because somebody's got to do the gift shopping and no way is it getting done while either of us is at work.

Can you say "Rut?"

Hey, it happens to the best of us. We get comfortable with one another, understand each other's grooves and fall lockstep into them as time in the relationship passes. We're content and not necessarily concerned with making anyone happy because, shoot, everyone's happy, aren't they? Bored. But happy.

Or so we think.

It's the kind of thing—The Rut—that can lead you to think that everything is just hunky dory and then—*kapow!*—the relationship is flushing right down the toilet. I'm not happy because you're not romancing me and paying attention to me and loving me like you used to. You're not happy because, dammit, your needs aren't being met, and your mind is straying and you'd rather be in a shiny red Porsche zooming down some country road with a former Ms. Black America than lying in the bed hugged up to my flannel nightgown yet another night. The kids are taking up the time that work doesn't, and we're just not taking into consideration that all the things that made us fall in love are missing, because they're hidden behind The Rut.

We sistahs notice it, but we deal. Love, I think, evolves for us; we recognize that the relationship is going to move from spring to summer to fall, with winter (the bad times) rearing its ugly head every once in a while, but nothing so serious that we can't expect to move into the next season of our lives. But, brothers—we're not sure you notice until it's too late, and you're ready to either burst or skip. So help us out: **When a relationship falls into a rut, do you recognize or care about it?**

From a Brother

We get there eventually, but it might take longer before we recognize that we're surrounded by a rut. When we do recognize it, we become extremely worried because we know this: If it's come to our attention, you probably got there a long time ago and possibly have already decided, by yourself, what you're going to do about it. We might not like your solution at all.

By their very definition, ruts are routines that one day became boring and unbearable. When you're sitting in the rut, all you see are the walls and ceiling you always see. Why can't a rut look a little different so we'd recognize the damn thing? And if ruts are routines, already that presents a problem because men like routines (yes, just like small children, so what?). They are soothing, comforting; they make us feel in control of our world, even if we aren't. For black men, who are not likely to be in control of their world during the workday, a home routine is especially welcoming. We know exactly what to expect when we pass through the front door. We can just feel the stress slide off our shoulders. We even grow upset if the routine has been altered in some way.

But what happens when this routine has become the epitome of stale and boring? Where does it lead us when our other half thinks our prized routine is the bane of her existence? She might want to spice things up—"Hey, how 'bout we do it tonight on the living room floor?"—and we look at her like she's lost her mind 'cause doing it on the living room floor before 11:30 P.M. would mean that we'll miss the second half of the game (since she surely won't let us leave the TV on) and possibly stain the living room rug that we just paid some guy $100 to shampoo a month before. That's a problem. It probably won't occur to us that the reason she wants to try the living room rug is because thrice-weekly bedroom sex in the same two positions at 11:30 has gotten kinda old to homegirl. It's comforting to us to know we're going to get some tonight at 11:30, and having to think of new positions in new places around the house three times a week would soon become stressful as hell.

Just like the subject of romance, we don't get into ruts on purpose. We get there because it doesn't occur to us that a rut has developed. We think of it as familiarity, and it makes us smile. Our women think of it as boring, and they grimace. Admittedly, we need some help.

Our ladies can do us a gigantic favor if they help us out of our ruts when they develop by suggesting new and interesting activities that they might want us to try. You wouldn't have to do this all the time—eventually we'd catch on and start coming up with stuff by ourselves. I say eventually, but each of us might have a different threshold for recognizing when our women are trying to jog us from routines. After their mates suggest a visit to the theater instead of a movie, and a sex session in the back seat instead of the bedroom, some guys might pick up the concept right away and run like hell with it. Next thing you know, home-boy might be installing a swing in the ceiling of the bedroom and putting video cameras in every corner of the room. Another guy might need to be dragged to the theater, the symphony, the opera and the ballet, plus come home to find a ceiling mirror and a guy named Jack in the bedroom, before he realizes his wife wants them to do more interesting things. I think we all deep down want our women to be happy; we just don't always know how to translate that desire into action.

Do women gain any comfort from routines?

From a Sistah

I think we all gain comfort from routine, because it means stability. It's the monotony that kills us.

We love going to church every Sunday, the movies on Friday nights, to Mom's house one Saturday a month, bowling every second Thursday. That's all right.

We hate eating tuna casserole on Tuesday, chicken on Wednesday, cube steak on Thursday, fish on Friday, out on Saturday (at the same restaurant), roast beef on Sunday and leftovers on Monday. That's not all right.

We love taking the kids to soccer practice every Saturday morning, going to the car wash every Saturday afternoon, making a monthly trip to the theater, shopping at our favorite store on Wednesday afternoon sale days, reserving Sunday morning between the hours of 8:00 A.M. and 9:00 A.M. to read the paper at the kitchen table. That's all right.

We hate going to the same club to listen to the same deejay spin the same tired records in the same order every week, hate eating at the same restaurant every time we go out, hate doing it in the same position in the same part of the house for the same amount of time at the same time every other night.

This is all to say that our routines don't have to be routine. There are some things that we have to do over and over again—and we recognize this. Mom is always going to want you to make time to see her, and if it works out better that you set a time with her so that you know not to plan anything else on her day, well, cool. The kid is always going to have to play soccer at the same time, the church is always going to meet on Sunday, the bowling league will always meet on Thursdays.

But in the times when we can clearly make a decision to do it differently, there's no reason why we can't be creative—to liven up things, or at least change them up a teeny-weenie bit.

That, however, requires effort—and for all intents and purposes, effort, in this sense, means romance. And effort, at the end of a long, tiresome, irksome day, is about as easy to muster up as it is to pick up an elephant with your pinky finger. It just ain't going to happen with the brothers because Number 1, y'all don't know jack bone about being romantic, and Number 2, y'all would rather cuddle up to a nice cold beer rather than be bothered with cuddling up next to us other than at designated, planned out and obvious times of the day.

We sistahs know it needs to be done—that we need to at least try—because if we don't we feel as if something is missing, as if we're approaching a dead end. We want to work ourselves out of the routine so that our relationships will work. There was a great line in one of my favorite movies, *love jones,* where the main character describes romance as the time between when you first ask her out and when you first make love—when you ask her to marry you and when she says, "I do." "When a person says the romance is gone?" he says with a shake of his head. "Nah, they mean they've exhausted the possibility."

Routine exhausts the possibilities—and exhausted possibilities means we're being denied the romance. We've already talked about how important romance is to a sistah. We also know that if we're stuck in a rut, it's just a matter of time before you all look up and realize your life sucks.

And what's the first thing you all do?

Lose your minds.

We want to avoid that, whether it be real or imagined. In fact, perhaps you can answer this: **Isn't it The Rut that leads men into the dreaded "midlife crisis"?**

From a Brother

Nah, it's the fear of dying that leads men into midlife crises. The tug of gravity on various body parts, the disappearance of hair on others, the disturbing appearance of too much hair on still others— like jutting from the nose and ears—these are phenomena that lead men to buy a red Porsche two-seater and screech around town look- ing for women barely out of their training bras to prove that we're not one step out of the grave. But since my "midlife" is so many years away, I'm just guessing.

Even though I'm not quite there yet, I'm already starting to understand the midlife crisis. My understanding comes from the mirror, the basketball court and Michael Jordan. I simply have a hard time understanding why weight refuses to drop from my frame even if I step up the exercise and lower the calories. Why am I not seeing a slender, well-toned body appear in the mirror before my eyes, just as I used to when I was younger and decided to drop a few pounds? And what happened to my first step? Mi- chael Jordan is about three years older than me—how does he still have a first step? My wife offers me answers to all these ques- tions—such as the idiocy of trying to compare myself in any way to His Airness—but what sits there wedged behind every question is the knowledge that from here on in it will only get worse. Gravity will only grow stronger in its pull, my first step will become even more nonexistent with each passing month, and the mirror will become more unkind and unforgiving. These are all the things I have to look forward to. In other words, I'm about to look down the other side of the slippery slope, that ominous peak that represents our physical selves. The view is scary as hell. Down there at the bottom I can see hearing aids, prostate trouble, high blood pressure. I don't see any tennis racquets down there, or any basketball rims. No pickup games, no marathon softball afternoons. (Maybe a few golf clubs.) That's what I'm staring at.

Right about now a red Porsche is looking pretty sweet. And I hear they have an awesome first step.

Acknowledgments

We humbly offer thanks to God, from whom all these blessings truly flow. You are a constant source of strength and light that continues to shine upon our path. We are forever gracious.

Many gigantic thanks to the two couples who have been demonstrating for us how this relationship thing is supposed to work for the past thirty-four and forty years, respectively: our parents, Bettye and Jimmy Millner, and Migozo and Chikuyu Chiles. You have instilled in us the family values others only talk about. We give you as noisy a shout out as is possible in print: WE LOVE YOU!

To Mazi: Watching you sprout brings constant joy.

To our siblings, Angelou, Jameelah and Troy: Siblings as best friends and confidantes—what a deal! And to our siblings-in-law, James and Ndegwa: Y'all the bomb. Our kinfolk sure know how to pick 'em.

Thanks to Valerie Wilson Wesley for the great idea. We owe you $10 and a great big hug. Also, thanks to Eileen Cope, agent extraordinaire, and Doris Cooper, an editor with a caring touch and the patience of Job, and all of our friends—who are way too numerous to list.

And special thanks to James O'Neal and the staff and students of Legal Outreach, and Shawn Dove and the staff and writers of *Harlem Overheard*. You continue to amaze and inspire us to always remain, in the infamous words of the ODB, "fo' da chilren."

Oh, and P.S.: This would not be a proper Denene Millner acknowledgment without special thanks to Stark and Jordan—my cutie-pie kitty-cats.